General Editor
David Piper

Titian

The Complete Paintings II

Terisio Pignatti

Art History Department, University of Venice

Translated by Judith Landry

GRANADA
London Toronto Sydney New York

Foreword by the General Editor

Several factors have made possible the phenomenal surge of interest in art
the twentieth century: notably the growth of museums, the increase of leisur
the speed and relative ease of modern travel, and not least the extraordina
expansion and refinement of techniques of reproduction of works of art, fro
the ubiquitous colour postcards, cheap popular books of colour plates, to fil
and television. A basic need – for the general art public, as for specializ
students, academic libraries, the art trade – is for accessible, reliab
comprehensive accounts of the works of the individual great masters
painting; this has not been met since the demise before 1939 of the famo
German series, *Klassiker der Kunst*; when such accounts do appear, in t
shape of full *catalogues raisonnés*, they are vast in price as in size, and beyor
the reach of most individual pockets and the capacity of most priva
bookshelves.

The aim of the present series is to provide an up-to-date equivalent of t
Klassiker for the now enormously enlarged public interested in art. Ea
volume (or volumes, where the quantity of work to be reproduced cannot
contained in a single one) catalogues and illustrates chronologically t
complete paintings of the artist concerned. The catalogues reflect as far
possible a consensus of current expert opinion about the status of ea
picture; in the nature of things, consensus has yet to be reached on ma
points, and no one professionally involved in the study of art-history wou
ever be so rash as to claim definitiveness. Within the bounds of hum
fallibility, however, every effort has been made to achieve bo
comprehensiveness and factual accuracy, while the quality of reproducti
aimed at is the highest possible in this price range, and includes, of cour
colour. Every effort has also been made to hold the price down to the low
possible level, so that these volumes may stay within the reach not only
libraries, but of the individual student and lover of great painting, so that th
may gradually accumulate their own 'Museum without Walls'. T
introductions, written by acknowledged authorities, summarize the life a
works of the artists, while the illustrations place in perspective the compl
story of the development of each painter's genius through his career.

David Pip

ntroduction

ne diet of German princes, convened at ugsburg in 1548, ratified a decision that was be crucial for Titian's future: it designated ilip II as successor to Charles V. During at winter the Spanish sovereigns had halted Milan, and Titian had been summoned ere to paint a first portrait of his future aster (No. 295). According to the de-ription in a sonnet by Aretino, this was a rtrait showing the sitter 'in a fine posture of gal majesty', that is, possibly standing, and med. It was sent by courier to Flanders, t then disappeared completely, since it seems ar that this was not the armed Philip II ich is in the Prado (No. 322) – possibly a plica of it – because there exist documents erring to the delivery of the Prado painting May 1555. In all probability the Prado rk was used as a letter of introduction from ilip to Mary Tudor of England, who was to come his wife in 1554. At all events the ado *Philip II in Armour* is an extraordinary rk, in its haunting play of colour with the ld-damasked armour against the table vered with deep red velvet. The face, with its pression of arrogance mingled with a ister melancholy, cruelly characterizes the ung twenty-three-year-old who was to eld such limitless and absolute power, and whose tormented person sensuality warred th a fanatical religiosity.

As if to confirm these contradictions, tian's work for Philip II was, from now on, separate into two strands: one distinctly otic, inspired by profane mythological *esie*, the other religious, devoted to the stere hagiography propounded and regu-ed by the Church. Particularly notable nong the mythologies are several outstand-g masterpieces produced for the occasion of e wedding with Mary Tudor, celebrated in England. The *Venus and Adonis* in the Prado (No. 338), painted in 1553, is the prototype of a series which includes numerous replicas: with its warm, evocative sunset lighting, it uses the suffused sweetness of its colours to express the deeply sensual feeling suggested by the meeting of the two young lovers. In 1554, Titian finished the *Danaë* (No. 342), now in the Prado, making use of the same figure of Danaë as he had used in the canvas painted for Ottavio Farnese (No. 255), but replacing the Cupid by an avid old woman collecting the shower of gold coins which are symbolic of her rape by Jove. Looking almost larger than life, her flesh pink against the white sheet, the shapely Danaë is reminiscent of Michelangelo (his figures of *Dawn* or *Dusk* on the Medici tombs) while the colour, which is dissolved into flashes of light, seems to reflect ecstatic physical abandon. The paint-ing undoubtedly represents a high point in the career of the painter, mature as he then was; and other canvasses of the 1550s bear witness to the freshness of his approach to profane subjects: one example of this is the *Venus at her Toilet, with two Cupids* (No. 345) in Washington, which presents us with an image of triumphant Venetian beauty, only mar-ginally tinged by Mannerist traits, for exam-ple, the red-green of the hanging in the background, or the elegant play of the two Cupids holding up the mirror. His female portraits, too, have an echo of the sensual power inspiring these paintings, and include the marvellous portrait of *Lavinia (so called) as Bride with a Fan* (No. 348) in Dresden, the *Venetian Girl* (No. 347) in Washington, and the *Lavinia (so-called), with a Tray of Fruit* in Berlin (No. 349): where dresses in a coral pink, light green and a superb golden-brown brocade give, each to its own compositions, its particular and positive splendour.

In his male portraits, however, Titian seems still to be relying on the established schemes of the previous decade, at most extending the structural range of his compositions. Often, the figures are seated in magnificent armchairs, as is the *Philip Seated wearing a Crown* in Cincinnati (No. 360), the *Ludovico Beccadelli* in the Uffizi (No. 331) and the *Portrait of Archbishop Filippo Archinto* in the Metropolitan (No. 362). This device allowed Titian to give greater emphasis to certain features of the figure, the red capes and white robes of the prelates or the damasked silks and gold chains of the princes. Sometimes Titian's strong dramatic sense prevails over the decor and this gives us, in the Thyssen *Francesco Venier* (No. 363), a powerfully expressive image of the old, sick doge. There the gold of the cloak seems to be in painful contact with the sharp rose of the curtain. The figure of *Cristoforo Madruzzo* in Sao Paulo (No. 330), painted in 1552, plays on a similar contrast of apparently clashing colours – the black of the clothing, the green velvet of the tablecloth and the red of the hanging. The unity of the masterpiece is, however, restored by the cold, frontal light.

The end of the sixth decade of the century was devoted to a very important series of religious works, many of which were intended for the court of the 'most Catholic king' Philip II. They were preceded by a huge painting on which Titian worked over a long period (from 1551 to 1554), the *Trinity* now in the Prado (No. 352). In accordance with a formula which was to be particularly successful in the Baroque period, various donors appear in the work alongside the religious figures: Charles V, the Empress Isabella, Philip II and Queen Mary. If it cannot truly be called a masterpiece, this great canvas demonstrates that the painter could, if necessary, adopt the formulas of a bigoted court, controlled by powerful 'confessors'. Titian's treatment of religious themes was much more successful when he could have free recourse to his own imagination. At times his religious feeling was to find expression in settings exceptionally filled by light, as in the *Annunciation* in San Domenico Maggiore in Naples (1557, No. 372) or in the *Pentecost* in the Salute in Venice (No. 373). Here, rays of light surround

the figures and give them spiritual value: t[...] angels melt away into flickers of gilded lig[...] the Holy Spirit sends down a rain of silver [...] the apostles, who appear trembling a[...] possessed. Similarly, in the *Crucifixion* [...] Ancona (1558, No. 377) and the *Christ on t[...] Cross* in the Escorial (1559, No. 382) t[...] figure of Christ stands out from the da[...] bluish background, while shafts of lig[...] illuminate the dramatic gesturings of t[...] pious women, or give a sinister quiveri[...] quality to the landscape of Golgotha, whi[...] becomes a landscape of death. The maste[...] piece of the period is undoubtedly the *Mart[...]dom of St Lawrence* in the church of t[...] Gesuiti (No. 380), on which Titian work[...] between 1548 and 1559. His tendency to s[...] his dramatic scenes at night, emphasizi[...] their movement through the dynamism of t[...] sources of light, seems completely develop[...] here. The use of colour, which is teased out [...] soft brushstrokes or thickened into carefu[...] calculated touches, also seems to be new. [...] short, here, at the beginning of his sixti[...] Titian seems to be embarking on what criti[...] have come to identify as his last perio[...]

During his last period, Titian's activity as a draughtsman assumed a dramatically pictorial character; he used both charcoal and pen to creat[...] strong contrasts of light and shade, as can be seen [...] the Mythological Couple Embracing *(Cambridge Fitzwilliam Museum) and in the* Landscape with Nude Woman Sleeping, and Animals *(Chatswor[...] Duke of Devonshire's Collection).*

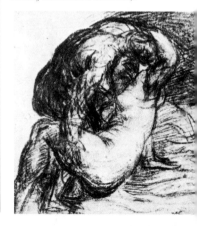

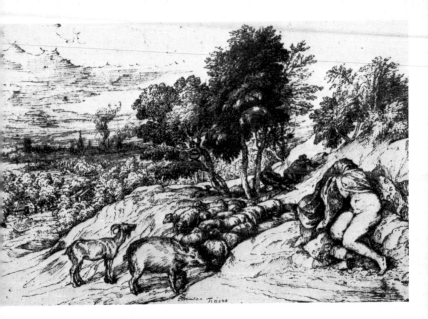

characterized by a mood of intense expressiveness. With Titian, there was no question of the effects of light being used as an end in themselves – as one sometimes finds, for instance, in the works of Tintoretto or the Bassano family. In Titian's painting the effects of light are closely bound up with the dramatic process of expression. St Lawrence is burning in the flames of martyrdom, and he himself becoming flame and colour in a sense that is at once mystical, spiritual and formal. He is symbol and sacrifice, an agonizing reality and a celebration of the pure values of form. Nor is it totally satisfactory to see his new style of Titian as fitting into the canons of Mannerism, however reasonable his suggestion might be when considering the experiences of the previous decade. In point of fact there is an existential presence prevalent in Titian's artistic ideals, an experience of feelings which go well beyond the invariably contrived elaboration of the *maniera*. One example of this can be seen in the painter's ability to impart a wave of near madness to the group of disciples in the *Entombment* sent to Philip II in 1559, and now in the Prado No. 383). Never, till that moment, had the sense of death and desperation been translated so forcefully into movement and colour.

Death and despair were feelings very real to Titian during those years. The year 1556 had seen the death of Aretino, Titian's companion for thirty years and his tireless champion in the courts of the powerful. In 1558 the Emperor Charles V died, a monarch to whom Titian was bound by affectionate gratitude and possibly by a bond of sympathy for the wretched events which had dogged the emperor's last years, in the solitude of the monastery at Yuste. In 1559 it was the turn of Titian's brother Francesco to die, a modest collaborator in so many artistic undertakings and an uncomplaining companion. Titian also had other reasons for worry and grief, in particular the attempted assassination of his son Orazio by the sculptor Leoni, who tried to lay hands on the two thousands ducats Orazio had just received in Milan as payment for the paintings sent to Philip II.

Tragic events, obscure presages of doom, saddened and haunted the now seventy-year-old Titian. Their weight can sometimes be felt in the beseeching letters he sent to a king, who gave no acknowledgement of the despatch of even the most stupendous paintings ('. . . it is now seven months since I sent your Majesty the paintings which you commissioned from me...') or did not trouble to ascertain if payments were made ('... I do not see how I can ever hope to obtain these payments' ...). The thought of death was woven into all his letters ('before I die ... now towards the end of my days ... this my extreme old age ... this stricken body ... the calamity of the present times').

The nature of many letters and documents dating from the end of his life have given rise to the myth of Titian's greed for money, and his miserliness. But it is surely quite clear that Titian was completely within his rights in demanding payment for his paintings – for which he undoubtedly remained in credit rather than in debit with the majority of his noble patrons. At all events, what is incontrovertible, and what interests us because it is closely linked to his artistic productions, is the sense of increasing depression and melancholy by which he was overcome, a sort of physiological premise for the twilight attitude which seems to be at work within his style itself. This had nothing to do with failing sight or unsteadiness of hand, as an over-positivistic school of criticism has imprudently claimed, but rather with the desperate and conscious rejection of life that was growing in the painter's increasingly weary soul. The Berlin *Self-Portrait* (c. 1562, No. 400) documents this moment most tellingly. The intervals in which Titian seemed miraculously to recover the creative inspiration and vitality of happier times were becoming rarer, though he could still sometimes respond to the ever-pressing requests for *poesie* for the secret *camerini* of Philip II. In 1559 he despatched the two great histories of Diana, now in Edinburgh (Nos 386 and 387), to Spain; a few years later he sent the *Perseus and Andromeda* (No. 407) and the *Rape of Europa* (No. 408). It is interesting to compare the mood of the first two paintings – intentionally erotic and still thematically linked to a somewhat outmoded classically-oriented culture – with contemporary Venetian painting between the 1550s and 1560s. The painter closest to these profane attitudes was possibly Veronese, working on the frescoes in the Villa Barbaro at Maser. But it seems very unlikely that there was any genuine point of contact between their Olym-

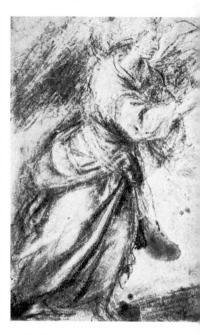

Angel of the Annunciation, *charcoal drawing, heightened with white, on blue paper (42 × 28) (Florence, Uffizi, Gabinetto dei disegni e delle stampe).*

pian beauty, emotionally cold and intellectually detached, and the deeply dramatic, and existentially involved, mood of Titian's fables. In the first of the two canvasses to-day in Edinburgh, Actaeon imprudently discovers Diana and her nymphs bathing, and his presence is like a hot storm wind suddenly unleashed, agitating the great crimson drapery against the green of the fountain. The rosy bodies of the naked nymphs weave between light and shade, and the shadow intensifies the modelling of the flesh, skimming it with a burning, sensual breath. There is surely nothing remotely similar in the equally naked but statuesque beauties of Veronese's Sala dell'Olimpo at Maser. There is a world of difference between the shimmering colour created by Titian's half-light, and the crystalline limpidity which clothes Veronese's forms in a transparency like that of an aquarium. Nor does there seem ny possible comparison with Tintoretto, though he, too, often painted nudes during his youth, for instance in the *Venus and Mars* (Munich) or the *Susannah* (Munich, Louvre and Vienna). Those images stress the dynamic and the linear and are intentionally remote from Titian's abiding vitality, which was to be far more tellingly taken up – in due time – by Rubens in the *Judgment of Paris* and by Velázquez in the *Rokeby Venus* (London, Wallace Collection and National Gallery).

Titian thus kept close links with the themes being considered in the first decades of the century, retaining his own particular brand of classicism, inspired both by antique statuary and by its reformulation of the time of Giorgione. But at the same time he knew how to breathe new life into otherwise antiquated iconographical themes (as one can see by comparison with the results when they pass into the hands of lesser painters, from Palma to Paris Bordone), a vitality which was connected with his hard-won emotional maturity, with the sadness of everyday living, the bitter consolation of the senses, his isolation in the world of memory and art. In our opinion this also explains the extraordinary quality of certain of his conceptions which, as in the *Diana and Callisto* at Edinburgh, anticipate, almost by centuries, later developments. They foreshadow the world of Watteau's *Fêtes galantes* or the decorative taste of a tapestry designed by Boucher, even more than they foreshadow Rubens. Titian also turned back to his past in his imagination but with what immense expressiveness! In his *Venus and Cupid with a Lute Player* (No. 402) at Cambridge, and in the contemporary version in the Metropolitan (No. 403), he makes, in fact, a virtual return to the *Venus and Cupid with an Organist* (No. 293) of some ten or more years earlier, but the rarefied and dazzling light in the background, and a certain *sfumato* softness in the chromatic touch, belong rather to the style which had developed between the end of the 1550s and the beginning of the 1560s. Thus the replicas of the *Venus and Adonis* of Philip II (see Nos 404 and 405) have a value quite independent of the original: that with a cupid added, now in the Metropolitan (No. 404) and the one in the National Gallery in Washington (No. 405) are much denser and softer than the earlier version, their *impasto* quivering with colour. Around the year 1560 Titian then devoted himself to three outstanding masterpieces. The Boston *Rape of Europa* (No. 408), completed for Philip II in 1562, carries broken brushwork still further; the forms seem as if continually striving to dissolve and reform in the misty atmosphere. It is rightly related to the *Perseus and Andromeda* in the Wallace Collection (No. 407). There, the eerily rippling waters are agitated by the approaching monster, while the beautiful figure of the woman makes her attempted escape in a diagonal, fleeing, as it were, towards the corner of the canvas. Lastly, we have the *Death of Actaeon* in London (No. 409), which was being worked on for Philip II as early as 1559 but which was undoubtedly finished later, extraordinary for the sulphurous flicker of light around the figure of the goddess, who is aiming her bow at Actaeon, mercilessly being savaged by the dogs.

These works established what was to be the expressive style of the last decade of Titian's work. Its reassessment is the pride of modern art historical criticism, possibly the most significant event in the history of Titian scholarship. Indeed, in sixteenth-century writings, as is well known, the late works of Titian had been regarded somewhat disdainfully. The Tuscan critic Vasari expressed explicit doubts about the *perfetione* ('perfection') of the *Annunciation* in San Salvador

The artist's signatures in the paintings here catalogued as Nos 320 and 344.

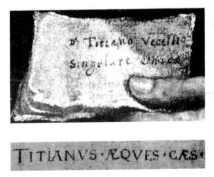

(No. 420), probably only just completed when he visited Venice in 1566, and also of other comparable works, since they appeared to him to be 'executed with bold, sweeping strokes, and in patches of colour', although he intelligently admitted that 'they appear perfect from a distance'. The Romano-Tuscan prejudice against the Venetian emphasis on colour, which apparently ignores design, long remained at the root of the incomprehension of Titian's late style. It continued throughout the whole neoclassical period and, summed up in the highly critical judgment of Cavalcaselle (1877–8), during the more positive 19th century. Yet a relevant page of Boschini (1674) recorded the invaluable evidence of a pupil of Titian's last years, Palma Giovane; evidence which should have served to explain Titian's highly original late style. When writing of the ageing Titian Palma recorded that he: 'laid in his pictures a broad mass of colours which served, so to speak, as a base' for successive stages of the painting, which was continually re-worked 'with bold strokes, with a brush heavily laden with colours; at one time with plain red earth for, as one says, the half-tones; at another with white lead; and with the same brush, dipped in red, black or yellow, he worked up the light parts; and, from these four strokes, by means of the highest Art, he could create a remarkably fine figure . . .' He continued: 'But the final touches he softened, occasionally modulating the highest lights into the half-tones and blending one tone into another with his finger; sometimes he used his finger to dab a dark patch in a corner as an accent, or to heighten the surface with a bit of red like a drop of blood. And thus he brought his figures to perfection; and in the last stages he used his fingers more than his brush.' It was not until the Impressionist painters won their battle against 19th-century academism that there was any appreciation of these perceptive words; it was then that the critics, having grown accustomed to their fresh approach, could look with new interest at its prefiguration, in Titian's late style. This was the discovery of Berenson (1894), confirmed by Dvořák (1927–8). Meanwhile Fry (1924) compared Titian's style significantly with that of the late Renoir, and Longhi (1925) and Pallucchini (1969) described Titian's development as

progressing from the 'chromatic classicism' o his early works, through an unacceptabl revolutionary Mannerism, to its final ou come in a 'chromatic alchemy' which – wit due regard for chronology – was defined as 'magical Impressionism', because of its com plete visionary originality. It was as if Titia had delved into some unknown depth to com up with an entirely new cosmic substanc from which to reconstruct his own hard-wo poetic vision.

The *Annunciation* in San Salvador i Venice may date from the beginning of th last decade of Titian's life, which starts i 1566 and ends with his death. Its frenzie brushstrokes seem to enflame the setting o the Madonna where the angels hover in th smoky air. Titian's vehement touch dissolve and recomposes the forms, which build up new principle of design. This (as in the stud for the Angel in the Uffizi) has been freed fror the sculptural and linear assumptions of th Romano-Tuscan tradition, in order tha through the interplay of repeated touches o tone and colour, pictorial form may b arrived at organically. One can well under stand the frequently adduced parallel betwee this masterpiece of deeply felt expressiv tension, and the late works of Rembrandt.

There are other works which, technicall and stylistically, correspond well wit Palma's description. In the Munich *Madonn* (No. 413) the figures, gleaming like phan toms in the foreground, are drawn from th shadows of a firelit landscape. Similarly, th little *Madonna* in London (No. 431) recalls with its delicate and melting *impasto*, th lovely *Madonna and Nursing Child* in th parish church in Pieve (No. 430). There is als the almost expressionistic reworkin (No. 432) of the *Entombment* previousl supplied to Philip II (No. 383), also in th Prado; and the reworking (No. 436), with it even greater insistence on the effects of light of the *Martyrdom of St Lawrence* (No. 380 for the Escorial, sent to Spain in 1567.

One might have thought that a period s intensely devoted to religious subjects, treate in such a wide, almost wild range of colour would necessarily have precluded any othe imaginative preoccupation, and have limite Titian's creations to a single pathetic mode But the ageing painter's extraordinary cre tive capacity is confirmed by the existence of many paintings, executed during the same period, which show an unlooked for independence in the treatment of mythological and profane themes. Thus we find a resumption of portraiture in the portrait of the Roman antiquary *Jacopo Strada* in Vienna (1568, No. 450). This is executed in scattered strokes, in browns and light ochres, against which the black velvet doublet with its red sleeves and the cloak of silver fox fur over the shoulders, stand out sharply. Close attention to the numerous details which indicate the subject's profession (the medals, the statuette, the cornice and the books) does not lessen the impact of the characterization of the face, whose gaze is directed questioningly out of the picture: a peculiarly modern device of a psychological intensity worthy of Shakespeare. And indeed the unassuming *Self-portrait* in the Prado (No. 458), with its old man's immobility, the eyes with their reddened lids gazing fixedly, the tremulous lips, the slightly unsteady hand clutching the still prestigious brush, seems inspired by a Shakespearean awareness, which is painfully human.

Lastly, there are, at the end of the seventh decade of the century, a number of mythological compositions: the *Cupid Blindfolded* in the Borghese Gallery (No. 438) with its partial replica in Washington (No. 439) is surely especially happy and characteristic of that 'unfinished' style which sometimes caused critical incomprehension. This painting, admired in Rome by van Dyck, who made a copy of it in his sketchbook, seems to envelop its mythological figures in a wave of crimson and gold: they look back to the happier style of earlier decades, but are now marked by something approaching existential anguish in the broken handling and the shifting colours.

Between 1568 and the beginning of the 1570s Titian also painted a series of figures of Christ, pious images of enduring pathos. At least three of these – the *Christ Blessing* (No. 452), the *Ecce Homo* (No. 454) and the *Christ carrying the Cross* (No. 456) – now in Leningrad – come from the Barbarigo Collection, which brought together the last works bequeathed by Titian, disposed of after his death by his son Pomponio. These are comparable, in theme and style, with another

Christ carrying the Cross in Madrid (No. 455), and with *The Tribute Money* in London (No. 457), sent in 1568 to Philip II for the Escorial. It is fascinating to imagine these small canvasses, all together in Titian's studio, being turned and re-turned to the wall, as was his custom, then worked on again, modified and retouched until they reached perfection; and to imagine the exacting Titian keeping them there until the last days of his life. They were in fact found together – a series of anguished faces silenced by pain – in his studio after it had been left empty for the last time.

The artistic relationship between Philip II and Titian, too, lasted until the very end: the famous letter in which Titian sums up the list of the latest consignments dates from 27 December 1574, while the one in which he makes his last request actually bears the date 27 February 1576: 'being already reduced to a very serious state and furthermore being in great need, in all humility I come to you to beseech you that, with your usual pity you might deign to give your ministers whatever order may seem most expedient for the relief of my needs. . .' Among the last canvasses sent to Spain was one of *Tarquin and Lucretia*, now in Cambridge (No. 460), and once again one is amazed by the quicksilver movement of the scene, which is emphasized by a very rapid, almost flickering play of light over the foreground. There is a probable first version (No. 459) of the work in the Academy in Vienna, executed with those 'dabs' which Palma saw as deriving mainly from the frenetic touch of the artist's fingertips. Two other works of the early 1570s, the *Adam and Eve* now in the Prado (No. 462) and the *Stoning of St Stephen* now in Lille (No. 464), are more monumental and oddly sculptural, possibly because they were conceived – according to the documents – considerably earlier and then abandoned, to be taken up again only much later. Here, in fact, the positioning of the figures is still Mannerist in type, but is not yet accompanied by the unmistakable pictorial touch of the later years, built up as it is upon changing effects of light.

The period around 1575 saw the delivery of other works which, for various reasons, had remained in Titian's studio over a long period of time: the *Faith Adored by Doge Antonio Grimani* in the Ducal Palace (No. 466), which recent restoration has returned to its wonderful intensity revealing passages by the artist's own hand, more particularly in the figure of the Doge; the *Religion Succoured by Spain* in the Prado (No. 470), altered from a previous allegory of Vice and Virtue, in which the complex, sensual forms seem to refer back to models of his youth, although these are taken up and retouched in the distinctive colour range of Titian's 'magical Impressionism'. The other paintings which conclude the catalogue of Titian's work must have belonged to the last months, if not weeks, of his life. At this point, while Venice suffered the horror of the plague, which was soon to enter his own house to carry off his beloved Orazio, we may imagine the old artist still obstinately going to his studio. Once again, perhaps, he may have taken down from the walls the canvasses of the *St Sebastian* now in Leningrad (No. 472), the *Marsyas* now in Kromeriz (No. 473), the *Nymph and Shepherd* in Vienna (No. 475), the mysterious *Boy with Dogs* in Rotterdam (No. 474). They are all works which were to be found in Titian's legacy, whence they passed 'into private collections in Venice to remain there for the most part until the seventeenth century, and this suggests that they had the same origin at the same time. They have a single stylistic theme, as though they were the supreme and dreadful expression of a soul drawing to the end of its days and driven to despair by the weight of age and the anguish of the moment. The colours become dark and nocturnal, with something faintly ominous in the feeble lighting; the glimmer of the reflections seems to summon a mysterious energy from the depths of the cosmos, like some ghostly offering made to the intensification of an image which was soon to fade.

The theme of light seems to recur desperately, almost symbolically in fact, in two very late canvasses: the *Christ Crowned with Thorns* in Munich (No. 478) and the *Pietà* (No. 479) in the Venice Gallery, intended by Titian to hang in the chapel of the Frari where he wanted to be buried. The light falls on the suffering Christ, as a shower of tiny drops of colour, which dissolve instantly, washed away over the surfaces, behind the shadowy folds of

the draperies, in the nocturnal depths. Ligh forms the figures of the last *Pietà* out of th recesses of silvery architecture vibrant wit golden reflections; it clothes the green an weeping figure of Mary Magdalene an makes the marble faces of the statues grimac weirdly, like gigantic ghosts. Everythin seems to quiver slowly, as though in th chromatic *largo* of some imaginary deat march.

After having sketched this panorama (Titian's work, one may wonder: what r mained of his artistic heritage after his deatl It is difficult to define the range of Titian influence; it was so vast and ramified. Thoug he did not leave a workshop, nor any re followers, he exercised a broad influence c almost all his Venetian contemporaries, fro Palma to Paris Bordone and Bassano. B according to Pallucchini (1969), who has dor considerable research on the subject, Titian influence was felt particularly by foreig artists, especially in Holland and German from Sustris to Calcar, Barentsz and Mo who had the good fortune to work in Veni in his sphere of influence. Then of course or must also take into account the worksho where his brother Francesco and his so Orazio worked, followed by his grandsor Cesare and Marco Vecellio. Then there a minor figures such as Gerolamo Dente, San Zago and Gian Paolo Pase who have prove interesting as far as clarifying attributions concerned, numerous spurious works havir been removed from the canon (see our list (attributions). In fact, it seems that the mo fruitful moment of Titian's influence was i the seventeenth century. It was then that showed itself directly both in Venice, in min figures such as Padovanino, and i ternationally, in the repeated contacts (Poussin, Rubens, Velázquez, Van Dyck an indirectly of Rembrandt with Titian's ar Many of these artists made copies of maste pieces by Titian. But most importantly, it wa by this means that the Venetian emphasis c colour passed into their paintings and becam a vital element in their art. This phenomenc demonstrates the perennial vitality of Titian style, certainly the most European in Venetia sixteenth-century art: a model which surviv until its reflowering in the astonishing chr matic sensuality of Renoir.

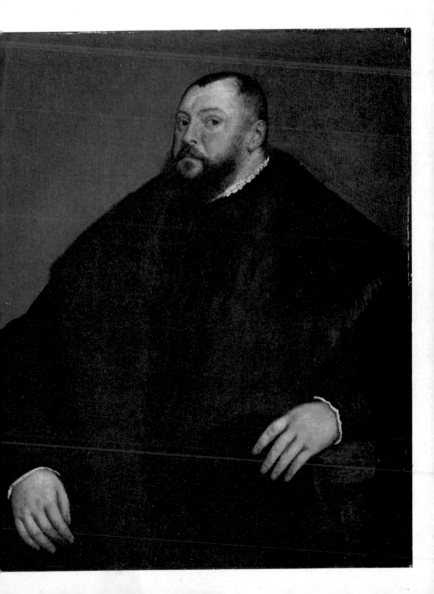

293 Venus and Cupid, with an Organist (W.III, 197)
Oil on canvas/115 × 210/S./1548–50
Replica of No. 281
Berlin, Staatliche Museen

294 Venus and Cupid with a Partridge (W.III, 199)
Oil on canvas/139 × 195.5
With assistants
Florence, Uffizi

295 Portrait of Prince Philip (V. 311)
Lost: documented *c.* 1549

296 Ecce Homo (V. 312)
Lost (letters from Titian to Granvelle 1548 to 1549)

297 Portrait of Lavinia Rangone (V. 313)
Lost: documented *c.* 1549

298 Portrait of the Duke of Alba (V. 314)
Lost: documented 1549

299 Portrait of Giuliano Gosellini (V. 315)
Lost: documented 1549

300 Portraits (V. 316)
Lost: documented 1549

301 Portrait of Queen Marie of Hungary (V. 317)
Lost: documented 1549

302 Portrait of Catherine of Austria (V. 318)
Lost: documented 1549

303 Portrait of Charles V (V. 319)
Lost (letter from Titian to Ferrante Gonzaga, 1549)

304 Tantalus (V. 322)
Lost: documented 1549.
There is an engraving of it by G. Sanudo (Photo 304a)

305 Portrait of Pietro Aretino (V. 534)
Lost: documented 1549

306 Tityus (W.III, 155)
Oil on canvas/253 × 217/1549
Madrid, Prado

307 Sisyphus (W.III, 156)
Oil on canvas/237 × 216/1549
Madrid, Prado

DUBROVNIK POLYPTYCH

(W.I, 168) (Nos 308A–308E)
Dubrovnik, The Cathedral
308A The Assumption
Oil on canvas/344 × 172/1549–50

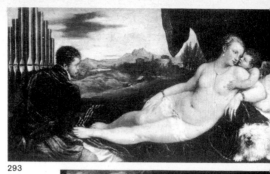

293

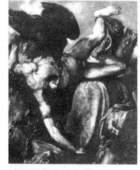

294

306

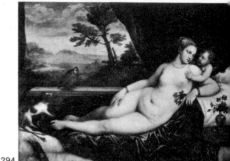

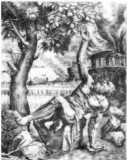

307

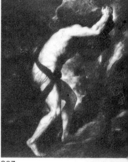

304a

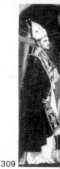

309

12

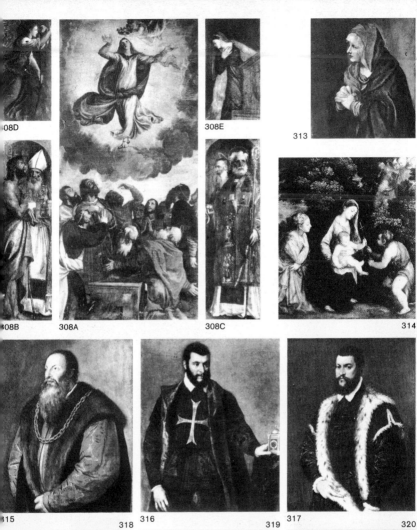

08D

308E

313

308B

308A

308C

314

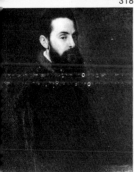

315

318

316

319

317

320

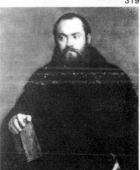

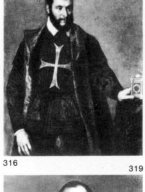

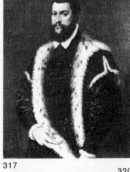

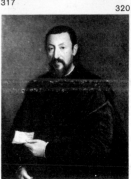

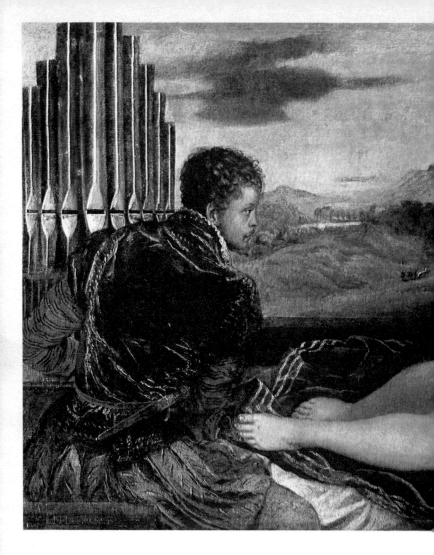

Johann Friedrich, Elector of Saxony, Seated (No. 321)
(p. 11)
The Elector of Saxony, leader of the Protestants defeated by Charles V at Mühlberg, was imprisoned in Augsburg between 1548 and 1551, and Titian probably made this portrait of him during that period; it shows an impressive figure, portrayed with splendidly imposing monumentality.

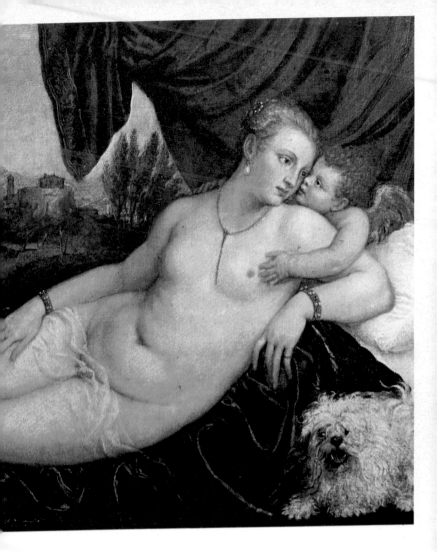

*enus and Cupid, with an
rganist (No. 293)*
*erhaps the prototype of a
bject repeated many times,
is canvas dates from about
548–50. It expressed the
ood of the profoundly
nsual civilization of Venice
the sixteenth century, a
vilization that was often
ithfully interpreted by
itian.*

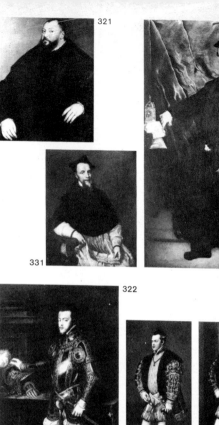

321

331

322

336

332

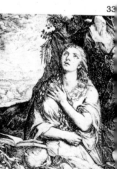

308B SS Lazarus and Blaise
Oil on canvas/200 × 55/
1549–50
308C SS Nicholas of Ban and Anthony
Oil on canvas/200 × 55/
1549–50
308D Angel of the Annunciation
Oil on canvas/100 × 55/
1549–50
308E The Virgin Annunciate
Oil on canvas/100 × 55/
1549–50
309 St Tiziano (W.I, 179)
Oil on canvas/182 × 59/
1549–50
Lentinai, Parish church
310 Self-portrait (V. 328)
Lost: documented *c.* 1550
311 Portrait of Philip (V. 329)
Lost (letter from Titian to Granvelle, 1550)
312 Portrait of Charles V (V. 330)
Lost (letter from Titian to Granvelle, 1550)
313 The Mater Dolorosa, with Clasped Hands (W.I, 115)
Oil on panel/68 × 61/1550 (?)
Madrid, Prado
314 Madonna and Child Receiving the Cross from the Infant John the Baptist and St Catherine (P. 295)
Oil on canvas/95 × 87/*c.* 1550
Milan, private collection
315 Portrait of Pietro Aretino (W.II, 76)
Oil on canvas/99 × 82/*c.* 1550
New York, Frick Collection
316 Knight with a Cloak (Supposed Portrait of a Knight of Malta) (W.II, 114)
Oil on canvas/122 × 101/
c. 1550
Madrid, Prado
317 Filippo Strozzi (incorrectly called) (W.II, 143)
Oil on canvas/115.8 × 89/
c. 1550
Vienna, Kunsthistorisches Museum
318 Portrait of Antonio Anselmi (W.II, 74)
Oil on canvas/76 × 63.5/
s.d./1550
Lugano, Thyssen Collection

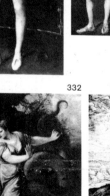

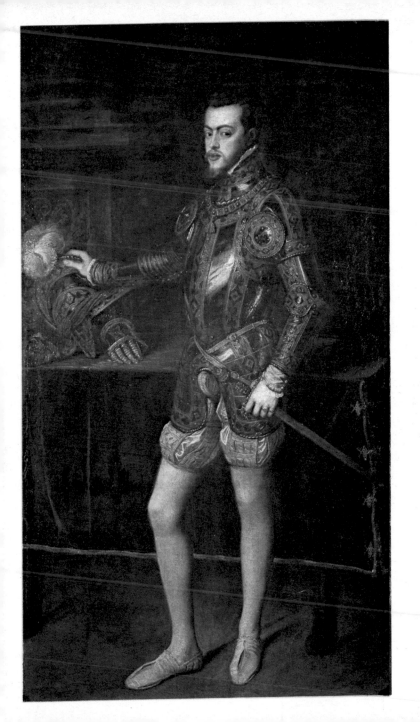

319 Portrait of a Franciscan Friar (W.II, 164)
Oil on canvas/83.8 × 73.7/1550–1
Melbourne, National Gallery of Victoria

320 Friend of Titian (W.II, 102)
Oil on canvas/87.5 × 70/s./1550–1
San Francisco, M. H. de Young Memorial Museum

321 Johann Friedrich, Elector of Saxony, Seated (W.II, 111)
Oil on canvas/103.5 × 83/1550–1
Vienna, Kunsthistorisches Museum

322 Philip II in Armour (W.II, 126)
Oil on canvas/193 × 111/1551
Madrid, Prado

323 Portrait of Guidobaldo II, Duke of Urbino (V. 348)
Lost: documented 1552

324 Queen of Persia (V. 546)
Lost: (letter from Titian to Philip II, 1552)

325 Landscape (V. 546)
Lost (letter from Titian to Philip II, 1552)

326 St Margaret (V. 546)
Lost (letter from Titian to Philip II, 1552)

327 Christ (V. 547)
Lost: documented *c.* 1552

328 Portrait of the Duke of Atri (V. 349)
Lost: documented 1552

329 Self-portrait (V. 350)
Lost: documented 1552

330 Cristoforo Madruzzo, Cardinal and Bishop of Trent (W.II, 116)
Oil on canvas/210 × 109/s.d./1552
San Paolo, Museu de Arte

331 Ludovico Beccadelli (W.II, 81)
Oil on canvas/111 × 98.5/s.d./1552
Florence, Uffizi

332 St Margaret (W.I, 141)
Oil on canvas/210 × 170/1552 (?)
Escorial, San Lorenzo

333 Portrait of Philip II (V. 353)
Lost: documented 1553

334 Portraits (V. 548)
Lost: documented 1553

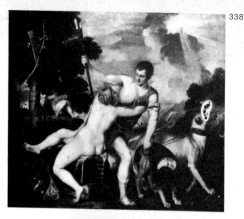

338

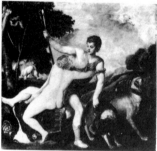

339

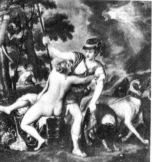

340

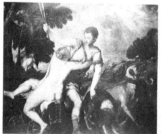

341

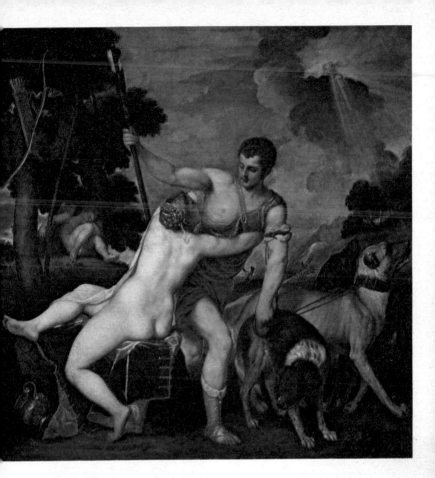

Venus and Adonis (No. 338)
Painted in 1553 for Prince
Philip, this is the prototype of
many versions of a poesia
which had a very popular
appeal, both for the sensual
theme and for Titian's dense,
fiery rendering of it.

**Philip II in Armour (No. 322)
(p. 17)**
This was painted in 1551 in
Augsburg, and is certainly the
finest of the many portraits
painted by Titian of Prince
Philip, destined soon to
succeed his father Charles V
on the throne of Spain.

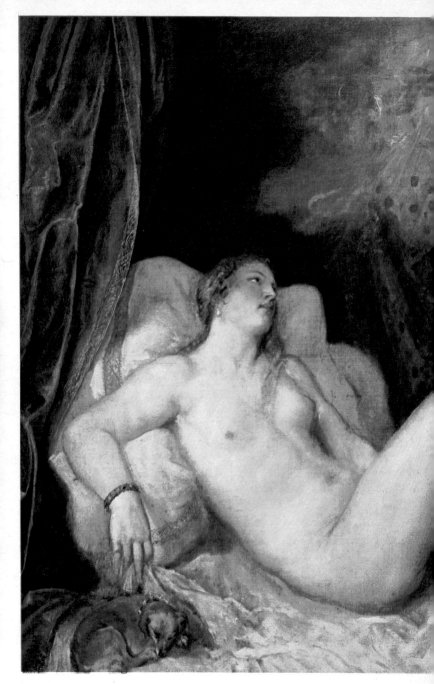

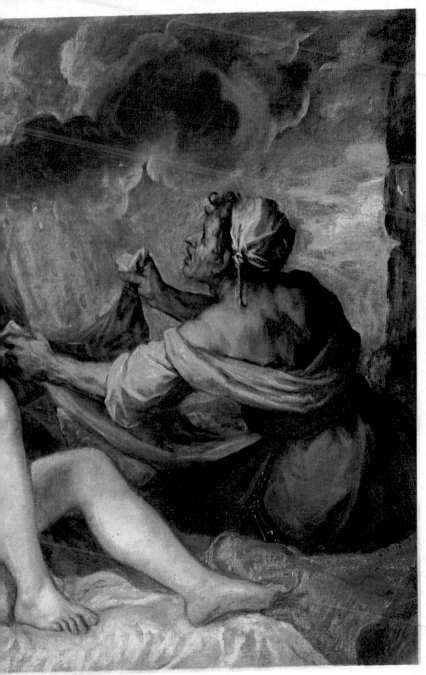

21

335 Mary Magdalene (V. 549)
Lost: documented 1553.
Engraved by C. Cort (Photo 335a)
336 Philip II (W.II, 128)
Oil on canvas/187 × 100/ 1553 (?)
Naples, Galleria Nazionale di Capodimonte
337 Philip II (W.II, 129)
Oil on canvas/183.5 × 100.5/ *c*. 1553
Florence, Pitti Palace
338 Venus and Adonis (W.III, 188)
Oil on canvas/186 × 207/1553
Madrid, Prado
339 Venus and Adonis (W.III, 190)
Oil on canvas/177 × 187.2
Replica of No. 338
London, National Gallery
340 Venus and Adonis (W.III, 223)
Oil on canvas/187 × 184
Replica of No. 338
Rome, National Gallery
341 Venus and Adonis (W.III, 191)
Oil on canvas/157.5 × 200.7
Replica of No. 338
Somerley, Ringwood, Earl of Normanton Collection
342 Danaë with the Shower of Gold (W.III, 133)
Oil on canvas/128 × 178/1553
Madrid, Prado
343 Danaë (W.III, 210)
Oil on canvas//119.5 × 187
Variant of No. 342
Leningrad, The Hermitage
344 Danaë with Nurse (W.III, 135)
Oil on canvas/135 × 152/s.
Variant of No. 342
Vienna, Kunsthistorisches Museum
345 Venus at her Toilet, with two Cupids (W.III, 200)
Oil on canvas/124.5 × 105.5/ 1553–4
Variant in Cologne
Washington, National Gallery of Art
346 Venus Alone at her Toilet (W.III, 222)
Oil on canvas/115 × 67/s./ 1553–4
With assistants
Venice, Ca' d'Oro

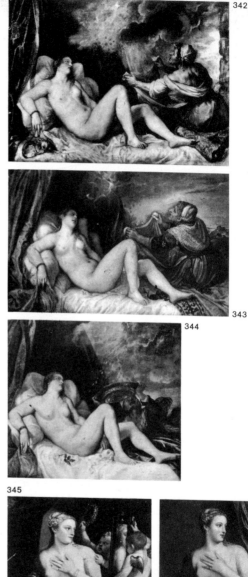

342

343

344

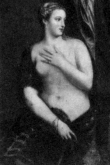

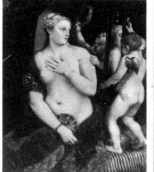

345

34

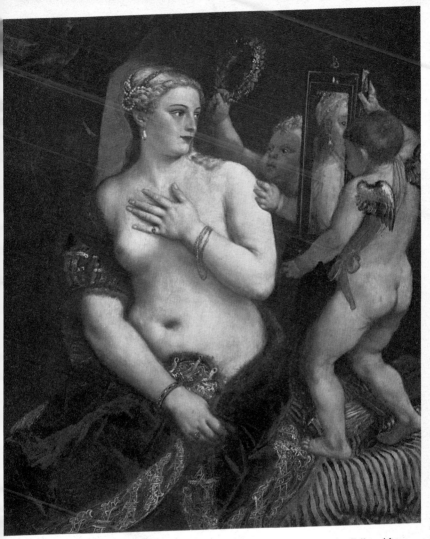

Danaë with the Shower of Gold (No. 342) (pp. 20–21)
This is a second version (with an old woman in the place of a Cupid) of the prototype painted for the Farnese family in 1546 (No. 255). This one, which was sent to Philip in 1554, seems to be in an even more intensely sensual key, with its golden colours and broken touch.

Venus at her Toilet, with two Cupids (No. 345)
Part of the 'legacy' Titian left at his death, this painting went to Leningrad and finally to Washington. The X-ray reveals a double portrait, subsequently covered over. A masterpiece of classical beauty, soft colour and velvety textures.

23

347 *Venetian Girl* (W.II, 186)
Oil on canvas//98 × 74/
1553–4
Washington, National
Gallery of Art
348 *Lavinia (so-called), as*
Bride, with a Fan (W.II, 114)
Oil on canvas/102 × 86/
1553–4
Dresden, Gemäldegalerie
349 *Lavinia (so-called), with a*
Tray of Fruit (W.II, 115)
Oil on canvas/102 × 82/
1553–4
Berlin, Staatliche Museen
350 *'Noli me tangere'* (W.I,
119)
Oil on canvas/68 × 62/1553–4
Fragment
Madrid, Prado
351 *The Mater Dolorosa, with*
Raised Hands (W.I, 115)
Oil on marble/68 × 53/s./
c. 1554
Madrid, Prado
352 *Adoration of the Trinity*
(Gloria) (W.I, 165)
Oil on canvas/346 × 240/s./
c. 1554
Madrid, Prado

347   349

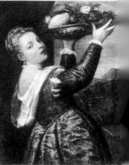

348

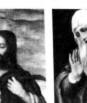

350   35

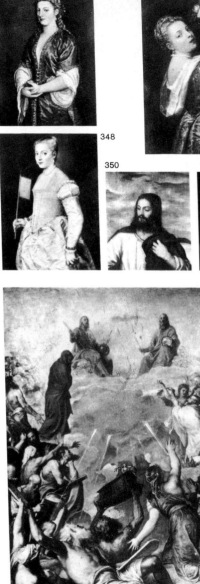

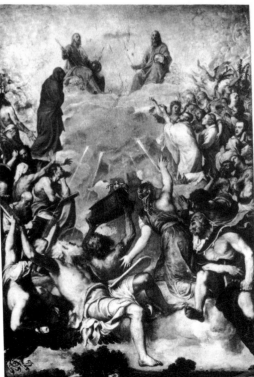

Venetian Girl (No. 347)
Believed to be a portrait of
Titian's daughter Lavinia, this
canvas is an unprecedented
harmony of golden and green
silks and of singular elegance.
The young face, painted in
delicate brushstrokes, emerges
from amid the silks.

352

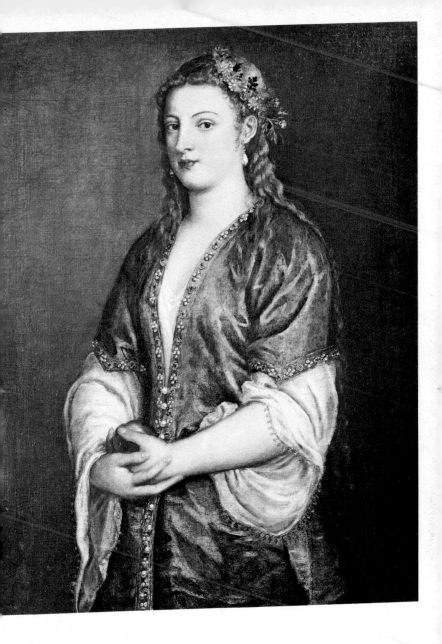

353 Apparition of Christ to the Madonna (W.I, 74)
Oil on canvas/276 × 198/
c. 1554
Titian and workshop
Medole, Church of Santa
Maria
354 Portrait of Francesco Vargas (V. 358)
Lost (letter from Titian to
Charles V, 1554)
355 Doge Marcantonio Trevisan kneeling before the Madonna and Child being presented by SS Mark, Anthony, Dominic and Francis (V. 363)
Lost: documented 1554
356 Portrait of Thomas Perrenot de Granvelle (V. 364)
Lost: documented 1554
357 St Mary Magdalene (V. 367)
Lost (letter from Titian to
Nicholas de Granvelle 1554)
358 Jason and Medea (V. 550)
Lost (letter from Titian to
Philip II, 1554)
359 A very pious work (V. 551)
Lost (letter from Titian to
Philip II, 1554)
360 Philip Seated, wearing a Crown (W.II, 129)
Oil on canvas/131.3 × 93.7/
1554–6
Cincinnati, Art Museum
361 Philip II Seated, wearing a Cap (W.II, 130)
Oil on canvas/96 × 75
Variant of No. 360
Geneva, Kreuger Collection
362 Portrait of Archbishop Filippo Archinto (P. 302)
Oil on canvas/118.1 × 94/
1554–6 (?)
New York, Metropolitan
Museum
363 Francesco Venier, Doge of Venice (W.II, 148)
Oil on canvas/113 × 99/1555
(?)
Lugano, Thyssen Collection
364 Venus (V. 368)
Lost: documented, c. 1555
365 Votive painting of Doge Marcantonio Trevisan (V. 376)
Lost: documented 1555.
366 Portrait of Alfonso I (V. 378)
Lost: documented 1555

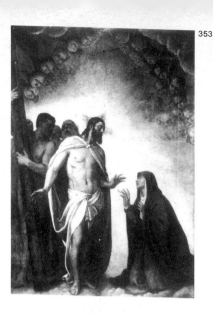

353

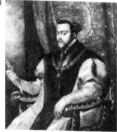

360

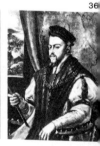

36

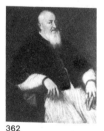

362

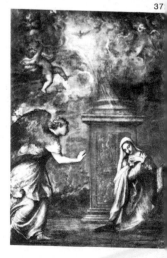

37

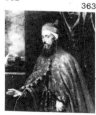

363

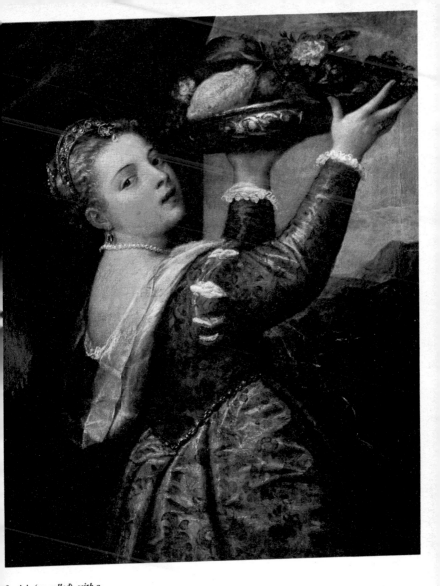

Lavinia (so-called), with a Tray of Fruit (No. 349)
A masterly example of Titian's most sumptuous style, this young girl – wrongly believed to be his daughter Lavinia – has a hint of the last echoes of a contrived Mannerist pose.

27

367 Ercole II (V. 379)
Lost: documented 1555
*368 Portrait of Doge
Francesco Venier* (V. 380)
Lost: documented 1555
369 Last Supper (V. 382)
Lost (Vasari, 1568: 1555)
370 Madonna (V. 390)
Lost: documented 1555
371 Deposition (V. 394)
Lost: documented 1557
372 Annunciation (W.I, 72)
Oil on canvas/280 × 210/s./
1557
Naples, Church of San
Domenico Maggiore
373 Pentecost (W.I, 121)
Oil on canvas/570 × 260/
1557–8
With assistants
Venice, Church of Santa
Maria della Salute
374 St Jerome in Penitence
(W.I, 135)
Oil on canvas/235 × 125/s./
1557–8
Milan, Brera Gallery

*Mater Dolorosa, with Raised
Hands (No. 351)*
*This was sent to Charles V in
1554, and has the rare
characteristic of being painted
on marble. To its simple
colour scheme of three colours
– plum, blue and white – is
added intense religious feeling.*

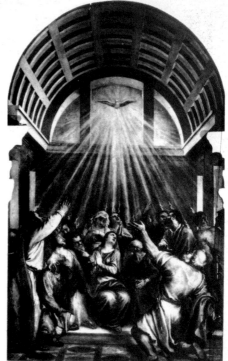

373

374

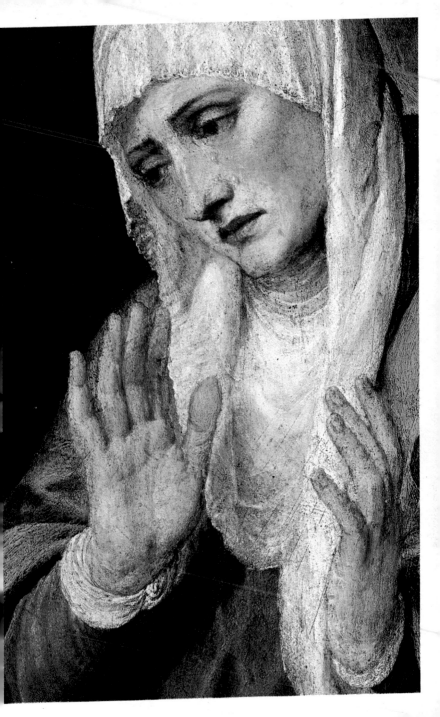

375 Fabrizio Salvaresio
(W.II, 137)
Oil on canvas/112 × 88/s.d./
1558
Vienna, Kunsthistorisches
Museum
**376 Standard for the
Confraternity of St
Bernardine** (V. 398)
Lost: documented 1558
377 Crucifixion (W.I, 85)
Oil on canvas/375 × 197/1558
Ancona, Church of San
Domenico
**378 Portrait of 'a young
Turkish or Persian girl'**
(V. 404)
Lost (letter from Titian to
Philip II, 1559)
379 Portrait of Philip II
(V. 554)
Lost: documented 1559
**380 Martyrdom of St
Lawrence** (W.I, 139)
Oil on canvas/500 × 280/c.
1559
Venice, Church of the Gesuiti

**Portrait of Archbishop Filippo
Archinto (No. 362)**
*Filippo Archinto, the
archbishop of Milan, was in
exile in Venice in 1554–5, and
Titian may have painted him
during those years. The picture
shows a firm, monumental
touch, befitting the dignity of
the sitter.*

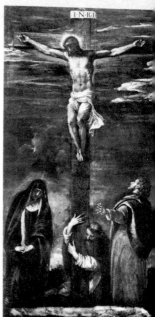

375

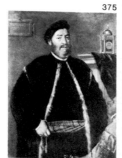

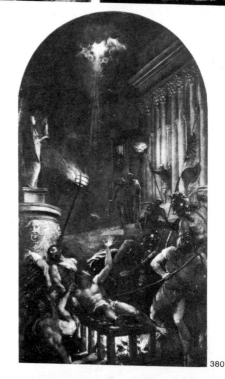

37

380

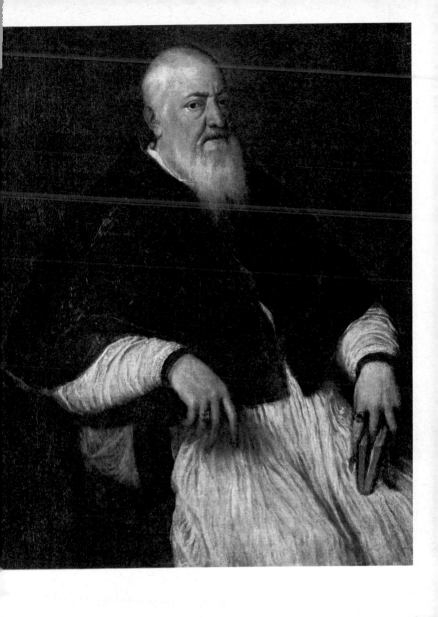

381 Ecce Homo (W.I, 87)
Oil on canvas/74.9 × 59.7/
c. 1559
Dublin, National Gallery of
Ireland
382 Christ on the Cross (W.I,
170)
Oil on panel/23.3 × 17/1559
Escorial, Nuevos Museos
383 The Entombment (W.I,
90)
Oil on canvas/137 × 175/s./
1559
Madrid, Prado
384 Adoration of the Kings
(W.I, 65)
Oil on canvas/138.5 × 219/s./
1559 (?)
Variants in Madrid, Milan
and Paris
Escorial, San Lorenzo
385 Adoration of the Kings
(W.I, 66)
Oil on canvas/112 × 213
Replica of No. 384
Cleveland, Museum of Art

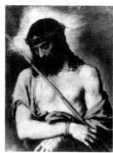
381

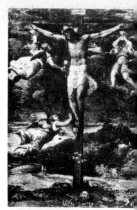
3

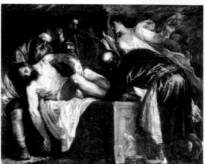
383

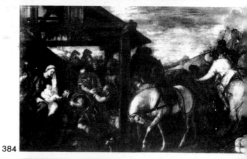
384

St Jerome in Penitence
(No. 374; detail)
Like a sudden apparition
glimpsed amid a grim
landscape of crags, St
Jerome clings to the rock, lit
by an unreal light, almost like
a fire which glimmers among
the trees and seems to burn the
limbs of the old hermit.

385

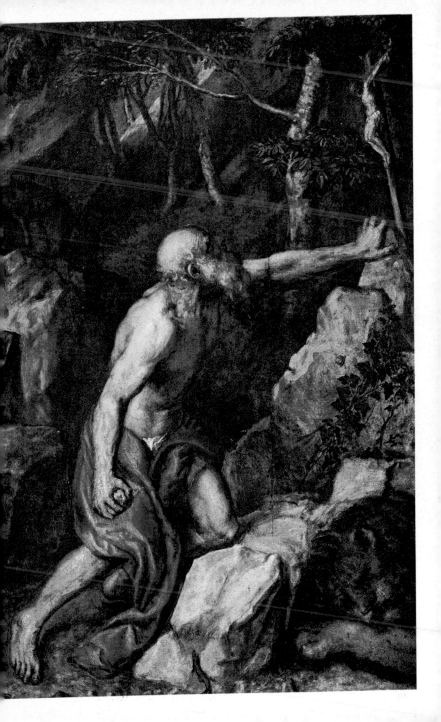

386 Diana and Actaeon
(W.III, 138)
Oil on canvas/190.3 × 207/s./
c. 1559
Pendant to No. 387
Edinburgh, National Gallery
of Scotland
387 Diana and Callisto
(W.III, 141)
Oil on canvas/187 × 205/s./
c. 1559
Pendant to No. 386
Edinburgh, National Gallery
of Scotland
388 St Margaret (W.I, 142)
Oil on canvas/197 × 167/s./
c. 1560
Kreuzlingen, Kisters
Collection
389 St Margaret (W.I, 141)
Oil on canvas/242 × 182/s.
Replica of No. 388
Madrid, Prado

Fabrizio Salvaresio (No. 375)
Of all Titian's portraits, this
one is outstanding for its
realism. As in other paintings,
the clock, here standing on the
piece of furniture, signifies the
relentless march of time.

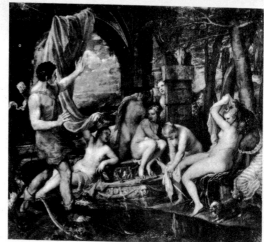

386

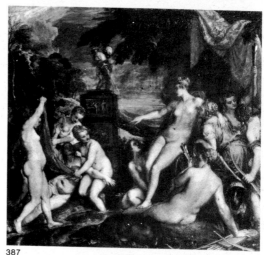

387

388

389

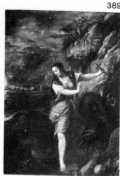

34

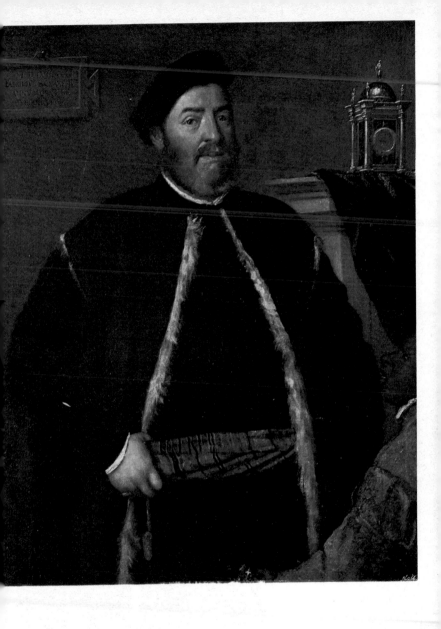

390 Wisdom (W.III, 204)
Oil on canvas/169 × 169/
c. 1560
Venice, Biblioteca
Marciana

391 Adoration of the Magi
(V. 421)
Lost (Vasari, 1568: 1560)

*392 St Mary Magdalene in
Penitence* (W.I, 146)
Oil on canvas/119 × 98/s./
c. 1560
Leningrad, The Hermitage
Variants at Busto Arsizio,
Genoa, Naples and Stuttgart

393 St Mary Magdalene
(V. 433)
Lost (Vasari, 1568: 1561)

*394 St Mary Magdalene in
Penitence* (P. 324)
Oil on canvas/109 × 94
Variant of the lost *St Mary
Magdalene* sent to Philip II in
1561 (No. 393)
Malibu, Paul Getty Museum

395 Antonio Palma (W.II,
120)
Oil on canvas/138 × 116/s.d./
1561
Dresden, Gemäldegalerie

396 Niccolò Orsini (W.II,
120)
Oil on canvas/87 × 70.5/s.d./
1561
Baltimore, Museum of Art

397 Man with a Flute (W.II,
117)
Oil on canvas/98 × 86/s./
1561–2
Detroit, Institute of Arts

***Martyrdom of St Lawrence
(No. 380; detail)***
*One of Titian's most famous,
and most tormented, paintings.
After being commissioned by
Vincenzo Massolo, he worked
on it over a period of eleven
years. It contains Mannerist
elements and reveals the
influence of Titian's stay in
Rome (in the background
temple, not included in this
detail). The main figures are
inspired partly by Mannerist
sentiments and are reminders
of the impact of Michelangelo's
work on Titian. Artificial
light, from the torches and
from the red coals of the fire,
plays on the body and limbs of
the saint.*

392
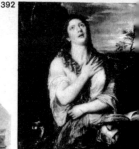

390
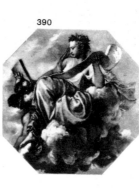

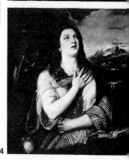

394
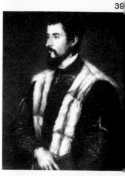

395
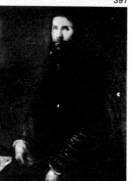

39

397

39
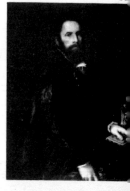

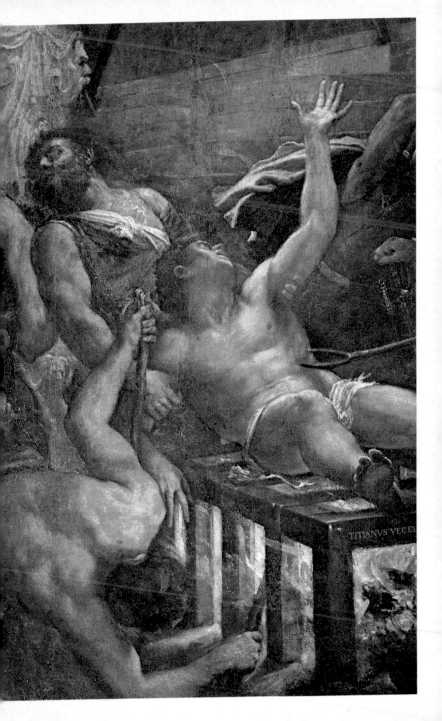

398 Antonio Galli (W.II, 165)
Oil on canvas/107.5 × 84/
1561–2
Copenhagen, Statens
Museum for Kunst
**399 Archbishop Filippo
Archinto** (W.II, 74)
Oil on canvas/115 × 89/
1561–2
Philadelphia, J. G. Johnson
Art Collection
400 Self-Portrait (W.II, 143)
Oil on canvas/96 × 75/1562
(?)
Berlin, Staatliche Museen
401 Unidentified Subject
(V. 555)
Lost: documented *c.* 1562
**402 Venus and Cupid, with a
Lute Player** (W.III, 196)
Oil on canvas/151.7 × 186.8/
c. 1562
Cambridge, Fitzwilliam
Museum
**403 Venus and Cupid, with a
Lute Player** (W.III, 195)
Oil on canvas/157 × 205
Replica of No. 402
With assistants
New York, Metropolitan
Museum

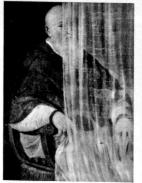
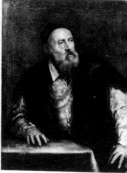

399

400

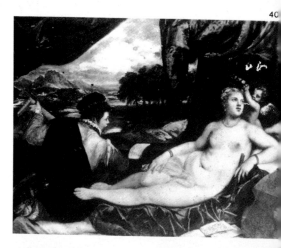

40

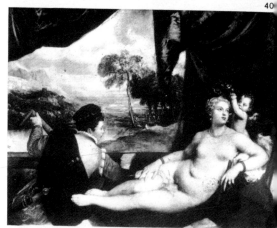

40

*Martyrdom of St Lawrence
(No. 380; detail)*
*The sinister, fiery light of the
torches and coals on which the
saint is being martyred lights
the scene, and glimmers
iridescently on the soldiers'
armour.*

38

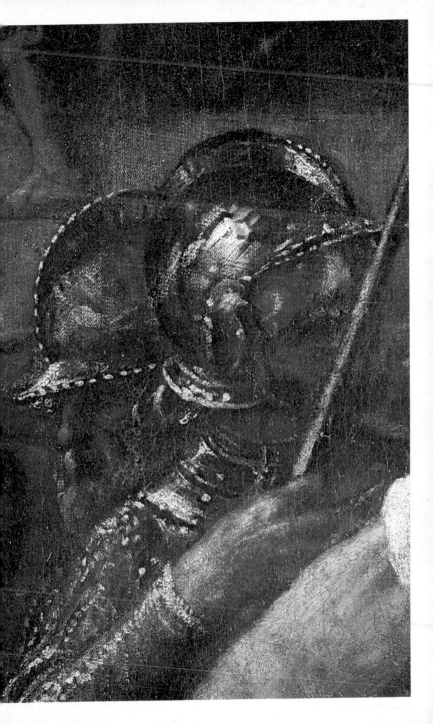

The Entombment (*No. 383*)
*Sent to Philip in 1559, this is
one of the most inspired of the
artist's religious compositions.
As though driven by a violent
whirlwind, the figures are
grouped in the shadow around
the body of Christ, who rises
from the great white patch of
the shroud. Titian painted
himself in the bearded figure of
St Joseph of Arimathea.*

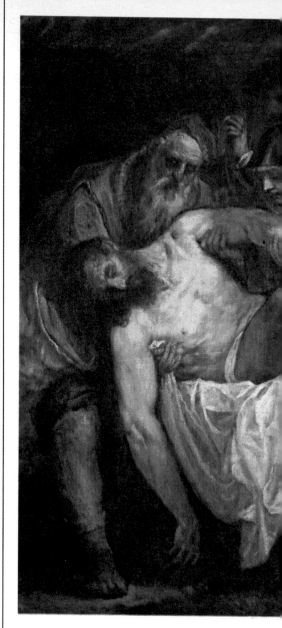

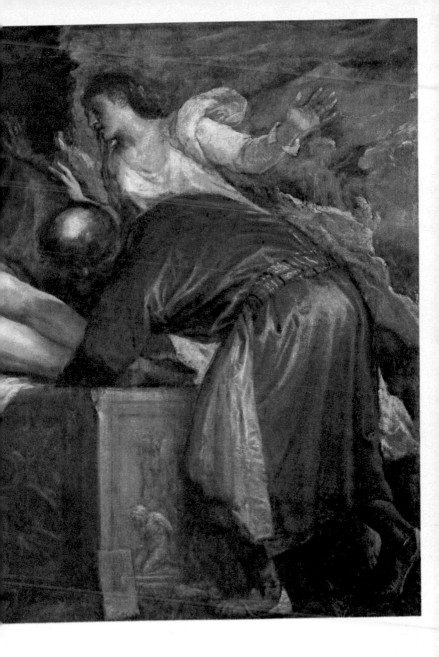

404 Venus and Adonis (W.III, 192)
Oil on canvas/122 × 135.5/
c. 1562
New York, Metropolitan Museum

405 Venus and Adonis (W.III, 193)
Oil on canvas/106.8 × 136
Replica of No. 404
Washington, National Gallery of Art

406 Venus and Adonis
(V. 556)
Lost (letter from Titian to Vecellio Vecelli, 1562)

407 Perseus and Andromeda
(W.III, 169)
Oil on canvas/179 × 197/
c. 1562
London, Wallace Collection

St Margaret (No. 389)
This is the last version of a theme tackled several times by Titian; it was probably painted during the 1750s. The intense, glimmering colour marks the tendency that was to become typical of his late works.

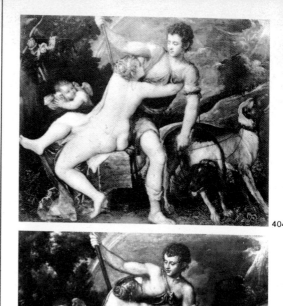

404

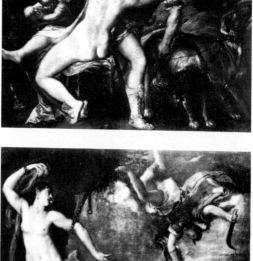

405

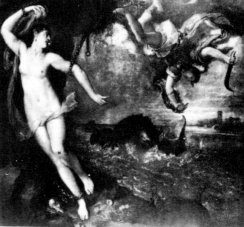

407

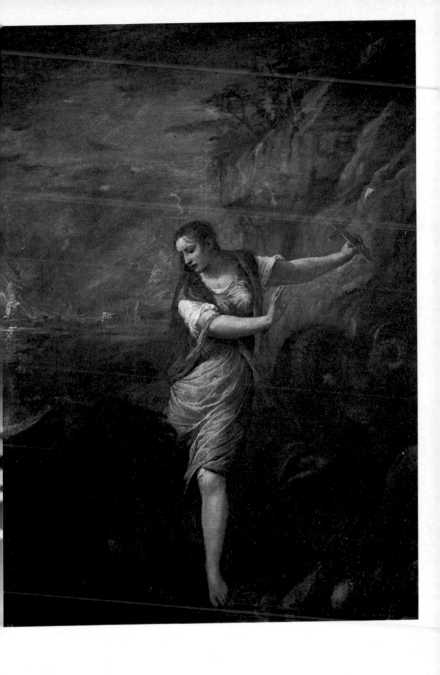

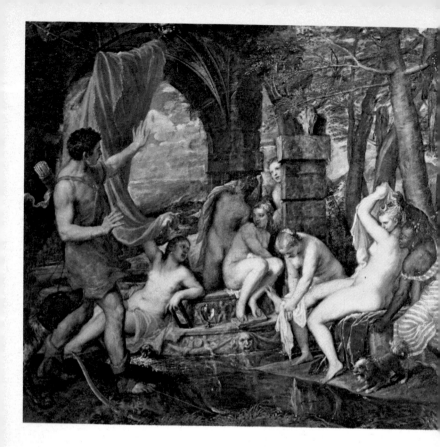

Diana and Actaeon (No. 386)
Sent to Philip II in 1559, this
great canvas marks the
beginning of Titian's last style
as it was to develop in his late
years. Though a work of his
old age, it can well bear
comparison, for its complexity
and richness of colour, with
the poesia sent thirty years
before to Alfonso d'Este in
Ferrara. Only the brushwork,
almost a short-hand with fused
strokes, is different, building
up the image by almost
magical effects of light.

44

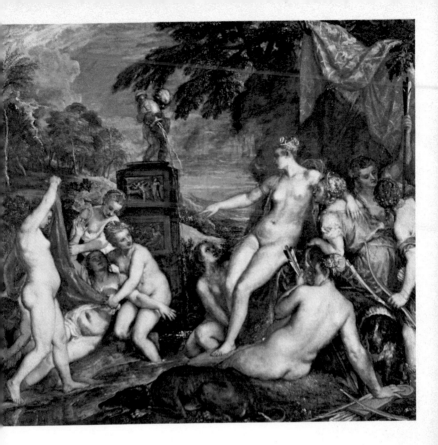

Diana and Callisto (No. 387)
A pendant to the previous painting, the Diana and Callisto *is a marvellously poignant and dynamic composition, like a great tapestry. It is a triumph with the bright, rich garments forming spots of colour among the nudes.*

45

408 Rape of Europa (W.III, 172)
Oil on canvas/185 × 205/
c. 1562
Boston, Isabella Stewart
Gardner Museum
409 Death of Actaeon (W.III, 136)
Oil on canvas/179 × 189/
c. 1562
London, National Gallery
410 Madonna (V. 557)
Lost (letter from Titian to
Vecellio Vecelli, 1562)
411 Agony in the Garden
(W.I, 68)
Oil on canvas/185 × 172/1562
(?)
Titian and workshop
Escorial, Nuevos Museos
412 Agony in the Garden
(W.I, 68)
Oil on canvas/176 × 136/1562
(?)
Titian and workshop
Madrid, Prado

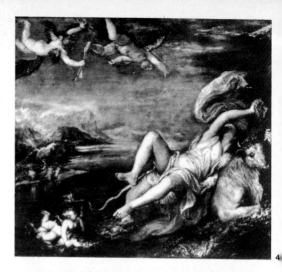

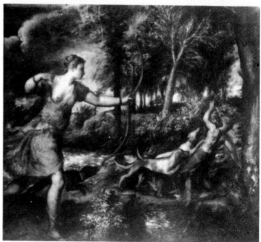

411

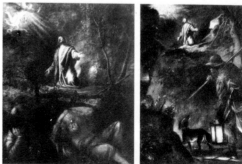

**St Mary Magdalene in
Penitence (No. 394)**
*Titian's youthful conception of
the repentant Magdalene
(No. 135) received various
later reworkings, including this
fine one in the Paul Getty
Museum; her pose is firmer
and her garments more clearly
drawn in.*

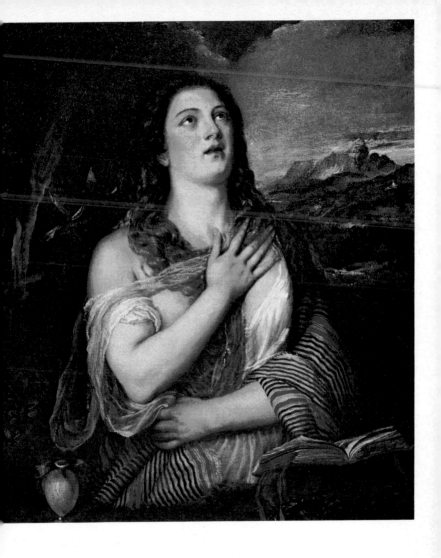

413 Madonna and Child in an Evening Landscape (W.I, 100)
Oil on canvas/174 × 133/1562 (?)
Munich, Alte Pinakothek

414 St Jerome in Penitence (W.I, 136)
Oil on canvas/184 × 170/s./ 1562–3
Escorial, San Lorenzo

415 St Francis receiving the Stigmata (W.I, 132)
Oil on canvas/295 × 178/s./ 1562–3
Titian and workshop
Ascoli Piceno, Pinacoteca Civica

416 Christ on the Cross (W.I, 85)
Oil on canvas/216 × 111/ 1562–3
Escorial, Sacristy

417 St Nicholas of Bari (W.I, 151)
Oil on canvas/171 × 91/s./ c. 1563
Venice, Church of San Sebastiano

418 Portrait of Philip II's sister (V. 447)
Lost: documented 1564

Self-Portrait (No. 400)
Vasari mentions a self-portrait by Titian, which he saw in his studio in 1566 and which is probably to be identified with this one in Berlin. The powerful figure emerges from the shadows, amid flickering lights which virtually dissolve the forms.

48

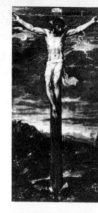

413

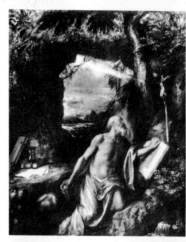

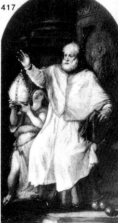

416

414

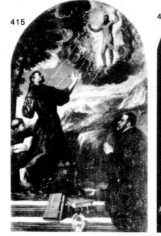

415

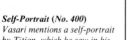

417

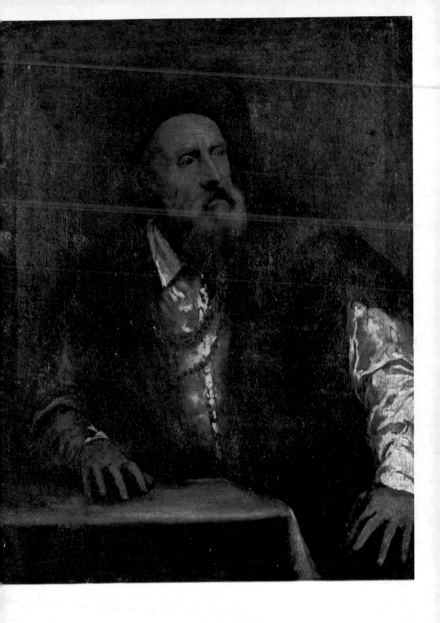

419 The Last Supper (W.I, 96)
Oil on canvas/207 × 464/s./
c. 1564
Titian and workshop
Escorial, Nuevos Museos

420 The Annunciation (W.I, 71)
Oil on canvas/410 × 240/s./
before 1566
Venice, Church of San Salvador

421 Madonna (V. 464)
Lost: documented 1566

422 Ecce Homo (V. 465)
Lost: documented 1566

423 The Crucifixion (V. 468)
Lost (Vasari, 1568: c. 1566)

424 Noli me tangere (V. 360 and 470)
Lost (Vasari, 1568: c. 1566)

425 Laying of Christ in the Sepulchre (V. 471)
Lost (Vasari, 1568: c. 1566)

426 Madonna (V. 472)
Lost (Vasari, 1568: c. 1566)

427 St Paul (V. 473)
Lost (Vasari, 1563: c. 1566)

428 Emanuele Filiberto, Duke of Savoy (W.II, 73)
Oil on canvas/223 × 151/1566
Kassel, Gemäldegalerie

429 St John the Baptist (W.I, 137)
Oil on canvas/185 × 110/
c. 1566
Replica in Novara
Escorial, Nuevos Museos

The Rape of Europa (No. 408; detail)
Completed in 1562, this masterpiece was also intended for Philip II. Against a sea of greenish-blue, and a sky darkly coloured with red and purplish gleams, the half-naked figure of Europa seems dissolved by the painter's open brushwork.

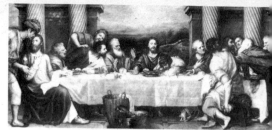

419

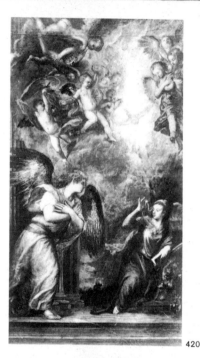

420

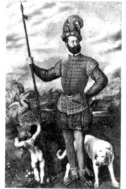

428

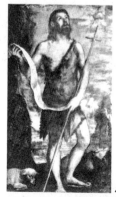

429

50

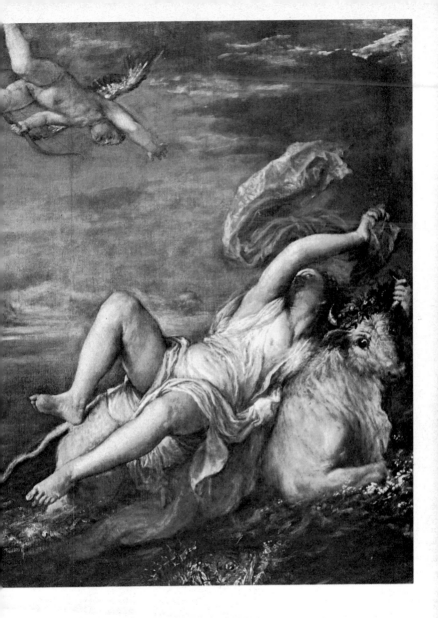

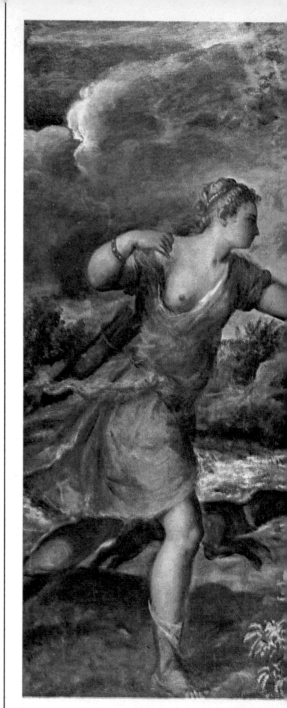

Death of Actaeon (No. 409)
Though mentioned in a letter to Philip II in 1559, when it was still being worked on in the studio, this painting was probably completed only during the following decade. The lighting of the landscape is the unmistakable proof of this.

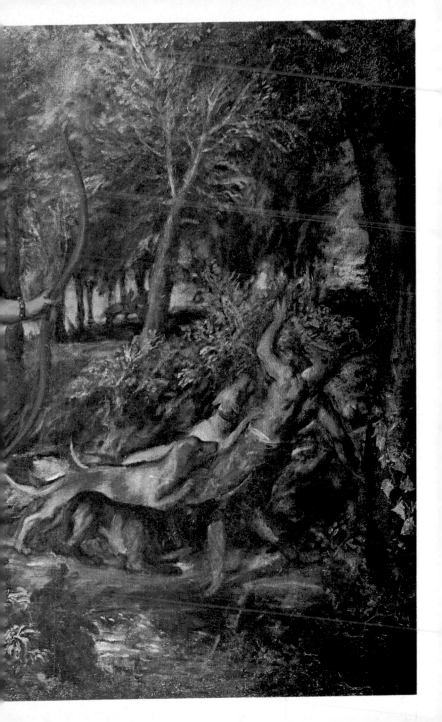

430 Madonna and Nursing Child, with SS Andrew and Tiziano, and Titian as Donor (W.I, 103)
Oil on canvas/100 × 140/ 1566 (?)
Pieve di Cadore, Parish Church

431 Madonna Nursing the Child (W.I, 101)
Oil on canvas/75.6 × 63.2/ c. 1566
London, National Gallery

432 The Entombment (W.I, 91)
Oil on canvas/130 × 168/s./ 1566 (?)
Madrid, Prado

433 Frescoes for the Parish Church at Pieve di Cadore (V. 475)
Lost: documented 1567

434 Nude Venus (V. 479)
Lost (letter from Titian to Philip II, 1567)

435 Madonna (V. 480)
Lost (letter from Titian to the duke of Urbino, 1567)

436 Martyrdom of St Lawrence (W.III, 263)
Oil on canvas/175 × 172/ c. 1567
Escorial, San Lorenzo

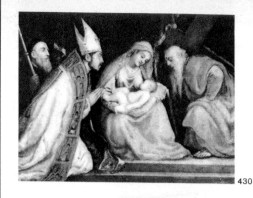

430

431

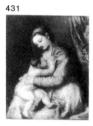

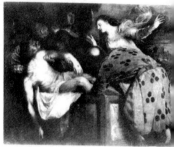

43

Madonna and Child in an Evening Landscape (No. 413)
In 1562 Titian informed Philip II that he had sent him a Madonna and Child, *which could be this one now in Munich. The figure of Mary emerges softly from the haze of a hot, dusky landscape, her dress transmuted by light into cloth of gold.*

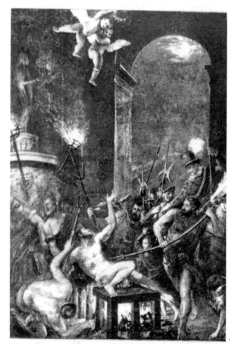

436

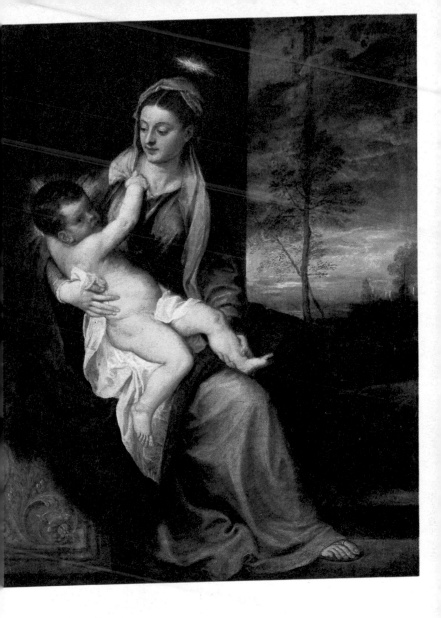

437 St Catherine of Alexandria in Prayer (W.I, 129)

Oil on canvas/119 × 99.5/1567 (?)

Boston, Museum of Fine Arts

438 Cupid Blindfolded (W.III, 131)

Oil on canvas/118 × 185/1567–8

Rome, Borghese Gallery

439 Cupid Blindfolded (W.III, 207)

Oil on canvas/122.4 × 97.3/1567–8

Partial replica of No. 438

Washington, National Gallery of Art

440 Salome (P. 318)

Oil on canvas/114 × 96/1567–8

Switzerland, private collection

441 Judith (W. I, 95)

Oil on canvas/112 × 93/1567–8

Detroit, Institute of Arts

442 Salome (W.I, 160)

Oil on canvas/87 × 80/1567–8

Madrid, Prado

443 Lavinia as Matron (?) (W.II, 116)

Oil on canvas/103 × 86.5/s. (?)/1567–8

Dresden, Gemäldegalerie

The Annunciation (No. 420)
This painting was seen by Vasari in 1566, and cannot have been painted much before that date. Vibrant with light, it has all the features of what has been called the 'magical Impressionism' of the late Titian.

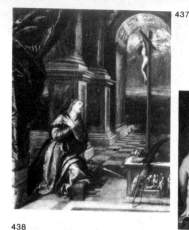

437

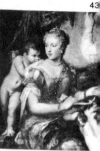

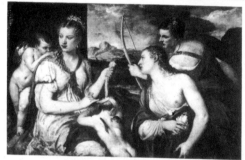

438

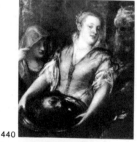

440

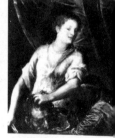

442

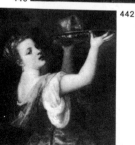

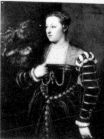

443

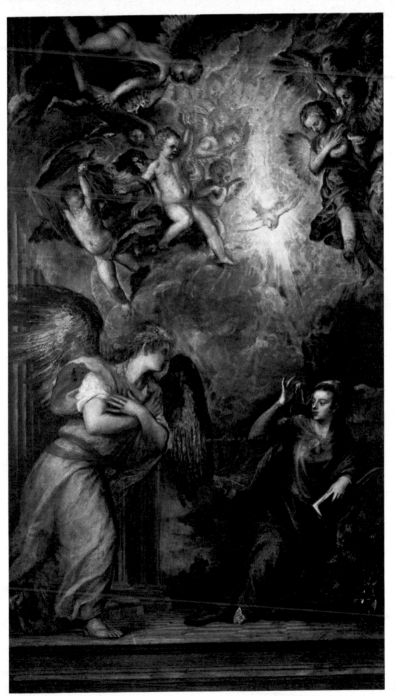

444 Paintings for the Town Hall of Brescia (V. 481)
Lost: documented 1568.
There is a drawing of them, *Brescia, Minerva and Mars* (Photo 444a), attributed to Rubens, London, British Museum; and an engraving, *Forge of the Cyclops* by C. Cort (Photo 444b)

445 Mary Magdalene (V. 482)
Lost (letter from Titian to Cardinal Farnese, 1568)

446 St Catherine (V. 483)
Lost (letter from Titian to Cardinal Farnese, 1568)

447 Death of St Peter the Martyr (V. 484)
Lost: documented 1568.
Engraved by Bertelli (Photo 447a)

448 Allegory of Religion (V. 485)
Lost (letter from Titian to Maximilian, 1568)

449 Seven mythological 'Fables' (V. 486)
Lost: documented 1568

450 Jacopo Strada (W.II, 141)
Oil on canvas/125 × 95/s./ 1568
Vienna, Kunsthistorisches Museum

451 St Dominic (W.I, 131)
Oil on canvas/92 × 78/c. 1568
Rome, Borghese Gallery

452 Christ Blessing (W.I, 77)
Oil on canvas/96.5 × 80.5/ c. 1568
Leningrad, The Hermitage

453 Ecce Homo (W.I, 87)
Oil on canvas/73 × 60/c. 1568
Sibiu, Muzeul Brukenthal

454 Ecce Homo (V. 463)
Oil on canvas/95 × 89/c. 1568
Leningrad, The Hermitage

Emanuel-Filiberto, Duke of Savoy (Wethey: Giovanni Francesco Acquaviva d'Aragone, self-styled Duke of Atri) (No. 428)
Identification of the figure has made it possible to date this impressive portrait to the last decade of Titian's life. In a great splash of colour, the costume stands out against the broadly painted, 'Impressionistic' landscape.

444a

447a

444b

451

452

453

454

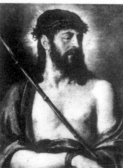

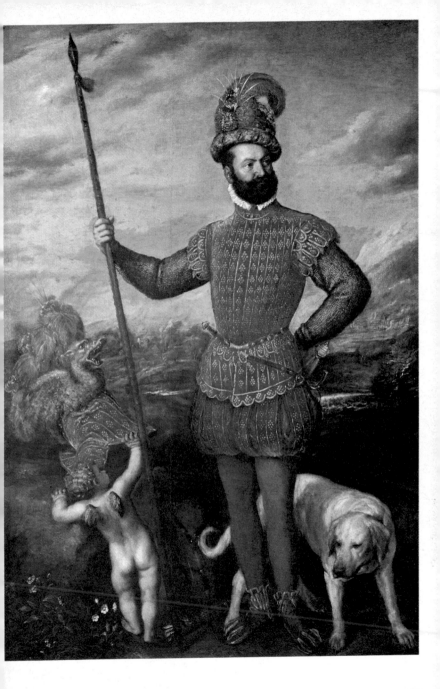

455 Christ carrying the Cross
(W.I, 81)
Oil on canvas/67 × 77/s./
c. 1568
Madrid, Prado
456 Christ carrying the Cross
(W.I, 81)
Oil on canvas/69.5 × 59.8/
c. 1568
Leningrad, The Hermitage
457 The Tribute Money (W.I,
164)
Oil on canvas/109 × 101.5/
1568 (?)
London, National Gallery
458 Self-Portrait (W.II, 144)
Oil on canvas/86 × 65/
1568–71
Madrid, Prado
459 Tarquin and Lucretia
(W.III, 220)
Oil on canvas/114 × 100/
1568–71
Vienna, Gemäldegalerie der
Akademie der bildenden
Künste
460 Tarquin and Lucretia
(W.III, 180)
Oil on canvas/188.9 × 145.5/
1571 (?)
Cambridge, Fitzwilliam
Museum
461 Tarquin and Lucretia
(W.III, 181)
Oil on canvas/193 × 143
Variant of No. 460
Bordeaux, Musée des Beaux-
Arts
*462 The Temptation of Adam
and Eve* (W.I, 63)
Oil on canvas/240 × 186/s./
1571–5
Madrid, Prado
463 St Jerome in Penitence
(W.I, 135)
Oil on canvas/137.5 × 97/
1571–5
Lugano, Thyssen Collection
464 Stoning of St Stephen
(W.I, 157)
Oil on canvas/194 × 121/
1571–5
Lille, Musée des Beaux-Arts
465 St Margaret (W.I, 178)
Oil on canvas/116.5 × 98/
1571–5
Florence, Uffizi
*466 Faith Adored by Doge
Antonio Grimani* (W.I, 93)
Oil on canvas/365 × 560/
c. 1555–75
Completed by Marco Vecellio
Venice, Palazzo Ducale

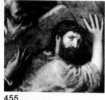
455

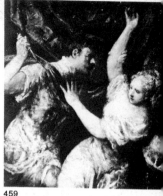

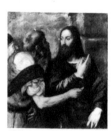
456

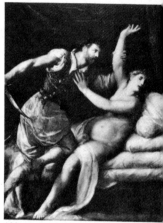
459

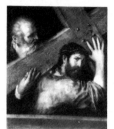
457

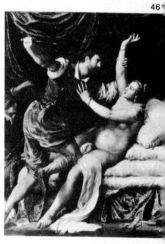
460

46

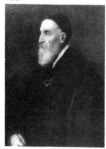
458

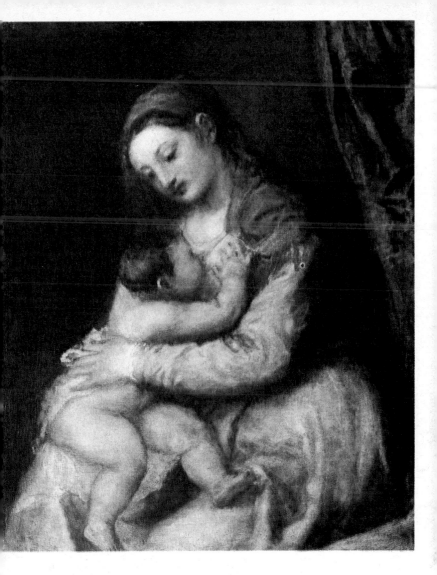

Madonna Nursing the Child
(No. 431)
Shaded indoor settings or
natural landscapes without
much light seem to have
inspired Titian mainly towards
the end of his life. In this
London Madonna, the forms
are hazy, defined only where
the light glances upon them.

467 Venus's Toilet (V. 507)
Lost (letter from Titian to
Philip II, 1574)
468 Nativity (V. 508)
Lost (letter from Titian to
Philip II, 1574)
469 St Jerome (V. 510)
Lost: documented 1575
*470 Religion Succoured by
Spain* (W. I, 124)
Oil on canvas/168 × 168/s./
c. 1575
Variant in Rome
Madrid, Prado
*471 Allegorical Portrait of
Philip II* (W.II, 132)
Oil on canvas/335 × 274/s./
c. 1575
With assistants
Madrid, Prado
472 St Sebastian (W.I, 155)
Oil on canvas/212 × 116/
c. 1575
Leningrad, The Hermitage
473 The Flaying of Marsyas
(W.III, 153)
Oil on canvas/212 × 207/s./
1575–6
Kromeriz, National Museum
474 A Boy with Dogs (W.III,
129)
Oil on canvas/99.5 × 117/
1575–6
Rotterdam, Museum
Boymans-van Beuningen
475 Nymph and Shepherd
(W.III, 166)
Oil on canvas/149.7 × 187/
1575–6
Vienna, Kunsthistorisches
Museum
476 Christ Mocked (W.I, 83)
Oil on canvas/110 × 93/
1575–6
Variant in Madrid
St Louis, City Art
Museum
477 Ecce Homo (W.I, 170)
Oil on canvas/84 × 112/
1575–6
Escorial, Neuvos Museos
*478 Christ Crowned with
Thorns* (W.I, 83)
Oil on canvas/280 × 182/
1575–6
Munich, Alte Pinakothek
479 Pietà (W.I, 122)
Oil on canvas/353 × 348/
c. 1576
Completed by Palma il
Giovane
Venice, Accademia

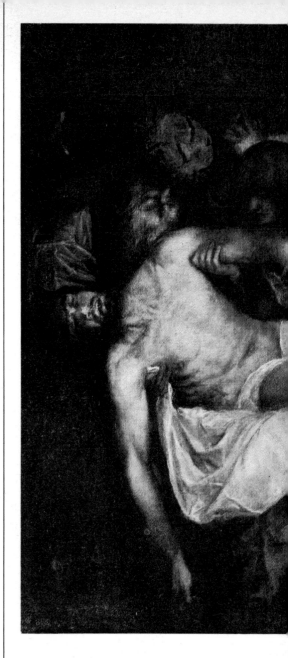

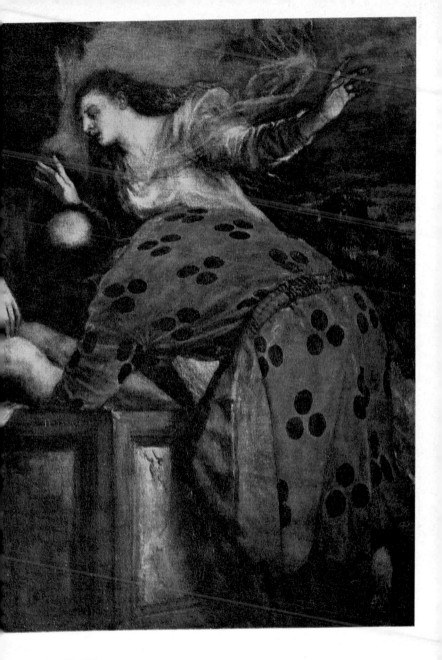

The Entombment (No. 432)

Taking the composition from a canvas of the previous decade (No. 383), Titian here presents almost the same figures, wringing from them, however, the maximum emotional effect. A nocturnal, almost lunar light, mysteriously touches the figures.

**480 Allegory of Prudence
(Titian's Self-Portrait with
Orazio and Marco Vecellio)**
(W.II, 145)
Oil on canvas/75.6 × 68.6/
1576 (?)
London, National Gallery

OTHER UNDATED WORKS MENTIONED IN THE SOURCES

(not illustrated)

INVENTORY OF THE VENDRAMIN COLLECTION (1567-9)

**481 Christ between two
Executioners** (V. 615)
482 Unidentified subjects
(V. 541)
483 Quarrel (V. 542)
484 Christ Mocked (V. 543)
**485 Portrait of a
Gentlewoman** (V. 544)
**486 Portrait of a
Gentlewoman** (V. 545)

G. VASARI, 1568

**487 Portrait of Francesco
Filetto and his Son** (V. 558)
**488 Portrait of Cardinal
Gonzaga, Brother of the Duke
of Mantua** (V. 559)
**489 Portrait of Giovanni
Fracastoro** (V. 560)
**490 Portrait of Doge
Leonardo Loredan** (V. 561)
491 Two Female Portraits
(V. 562)
**492 Portrait of Massimiano
Stampa, Commander of the
Castle in Milan** (V. 563)
493 Portrait of Nicolò Zeno
(V. 564)
**494 Portrait of a
Gentlewoman** (V. 565)
**495 Portrait of Francesco
Sforza, Duke of Milan**
(V. 567)
496 The Virgin Annunciate
(V. 568)
497 The Flagellation of Christ
(V. 569)
**498 Portrait of Francesco
Assonica** (V. 570)
**499 Rest on the Flight into
Egypt** (V. 571)
**500 Portrait of Giovanni van
Haanen** (V. 572)

462

463

46

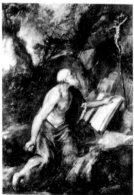

464

4

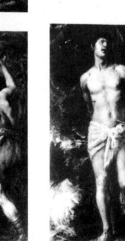

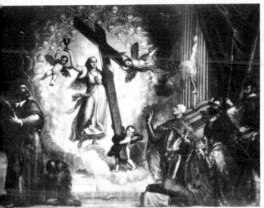

466

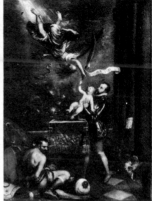

471

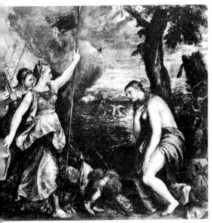

470

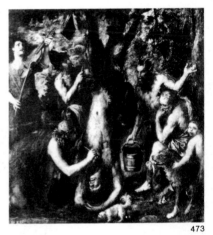

473

474

475

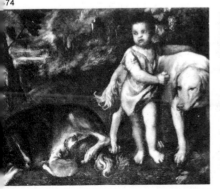

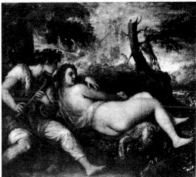

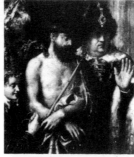

476

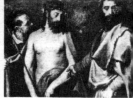

47

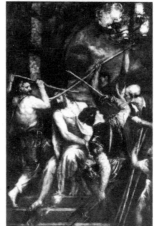

478

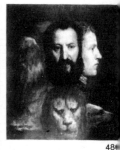

48

479

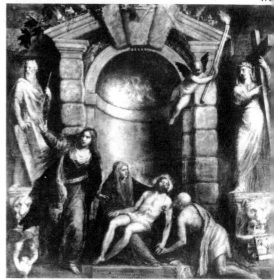

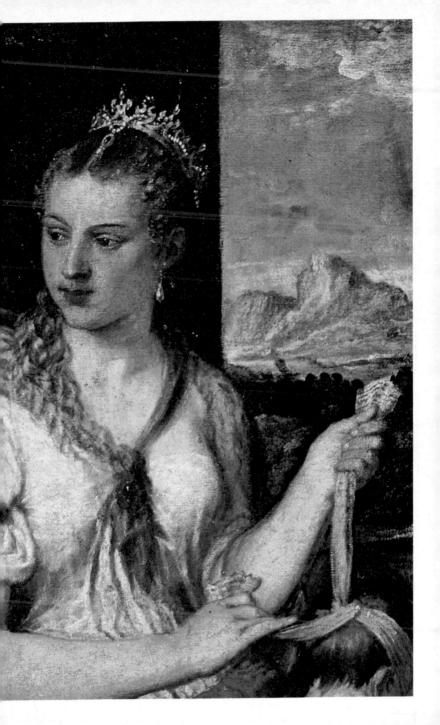

MAIN ATTRIBUTED WORKS

Attributed works are listed by collection in alphabetical order

519 Adoration of the Magi
(V. 582)
Oil on canvas/110 × 132
Aarburg, W. Lüthy
Collection

520 Giulia di Spilembargo
(W.II, 141)
Oil on canvas/72 × 48
Cesare Vecellio (?)
Andover, L. D. Peterkin
Collection

521 Pietro Aretino (W.II, 153)
Oil on canvas/58 × 46.5
Sebastiano del Piombo (?)
Basle, Kunstmuseum

522 Double portrait (V. 91)
Oil on canvas/87 × 102
Licinio (?)
Berlin, Staatliche Museen

**523 Nicholas Perrenot,
Seigneure de Granvelle** (W.II, 176)
Oil on canvas/122 × 93
Sustris (?)
Besançon, Musée des Beaux-Arts

**524 Christ on the Cross and
the Good Thief** (W.I, 85)
Oil on canvas/137 × 149
Palma il Giovane (?)
Bologna, Pinacoteca

**525 Madonna and Child, St
Catherine and Infant John the
Baptist** (P. 295)
Oil on panel/120 × 157
Bologna, private collection

526 Landscape with Figures
(P. 324)
Oil on canvas/59.5 × 81.5
Bologna, private collection

527 Gentleman with a Book
(W.II, 106)
Oil on canvas/97 × 76.5
Boston, Museum of Fine Arts

528 Franciscan Friar (W.II, 164)
Oil on canvas/66 × 57
Bowood, Marquis of
Lansdowne Collection

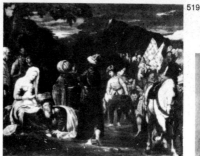

519

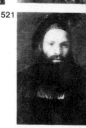

521

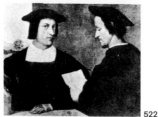

522

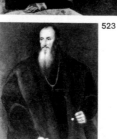

523

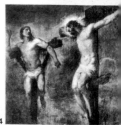

524

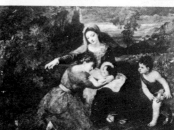

525
526

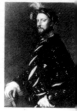

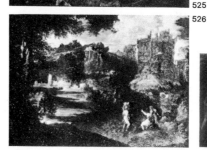

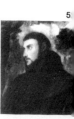

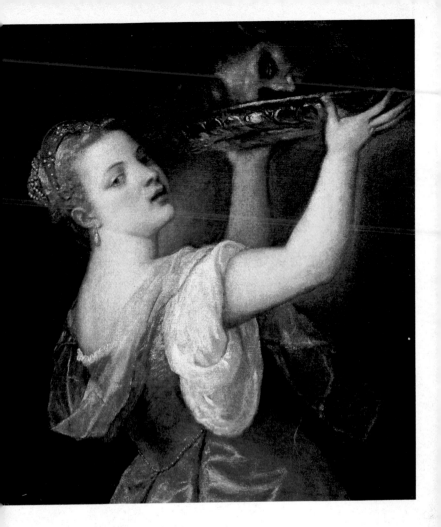

Cupid Blindfolded (*No. 438; detail*) (*p. 67*)
This scene of Venus blindfolding Cupid has only an apparent serenity. The brushstrokes, laden with stormy light, make the colour unstable and blur the design of the figures, which acquire a sense of subtle anguish, typical of Titian's late work.

Salome (*No. 442*)
Unjustly regarded as a doubtful attribution, this Salome should be placed among the master's late works.

529 Ostension of the Holy Cross (W.I, 177)
Oil on canvas/224.5 × 152.5
Moretto
Brescia, Pinacoteca Civica

530 Marcantonio Trevisan, Doge of Venice (W.II, 183)
Oil on canvas/100 × 86.5
Budapest, Szépmüveszeti Múzeum

531 Vittoria Farnese (W.II, 162)
Oil on panel/80 × 61.5
Budapest, Szépmüveszeti Múzeum

532 St Mary Magdalene in Penitence (W.I, 146)
Oil on canvas/105 × 92
Variant of No. 392
Busto Arsizio, Candiani Collection

533 Young Man with a Dagger (W.II, 189)
Oil on canvas/97.2 × 77.2
Cariani (?)
Chatsworth, Duke of Devonshire Collection
Not illustrated

534 Allegory of Cupid and Venus (W.III, 207)
Oil on canvas/129.9 × 155.3
Sustris
Chicago, Art Institute
Not illustrated

535 Danaë (W.III, 209)
Oil on canvas/121 × 170
Variant of No. 255
Chicago, Art Institute

536 Giulia Gonzaga Colonna (W.II, 169)
Oil on canvas/63.9 × 51.8
Chicago, Art Institute

537 Gentleman with a Dog (W.II, 168)
Oil on canvas/103 × 76.2
Chicago, John Maxon Collection

538 Antonio Galeazzo Bevilacqua (W.II, 155)
Oil on canvas/141.3 × 108
Cleveland, Museum of Art

539 Head of St John the Baptist (W.I, 178)
Oil on canvas/50 × 75
Cleveland, Museum of Art
Not illustrated

540 Venus at her Toilet with two Cupids (W.III, 201)
Oil on canvas/117.5 × 101
Variant of No. 345
Cologne, Wallraf-Richartz Museum

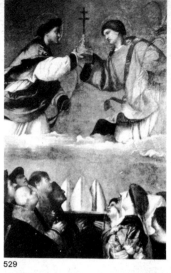

529

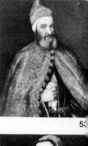

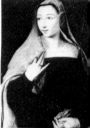

53

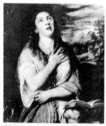

532

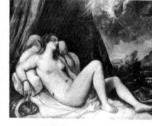

53

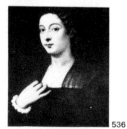

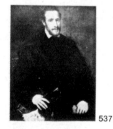

536

537

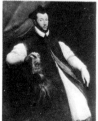

538

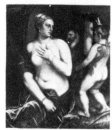

540

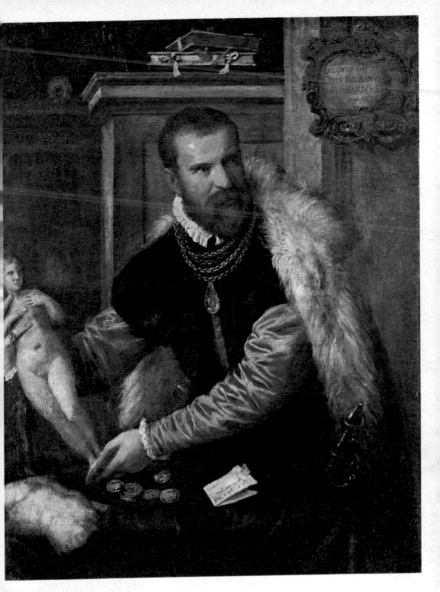

***Jacopo Strada* (No. 450)**
Probably completed in 1568,
the portrait of the famous
antiquary Jacopo Strada is
unique in Titian's late
production, both for the
originality of the conception
and for the touch, which has
once again become careful and
deliberate in the drawing of
the face and objects in the room.

541 Nymph and Satyr (W.III, 216)
Oil on canvas/99 × 80.7
Girolamo Dente (?)
Detroit, Institute of Arts

542 Andrea Navagero (so-called) (W.II, 175)
Oil on canvas/79 × 70.5
Detroit, Institute of Arts

543 The Appeal (Three Figures) (W.II, 152)
Oil on canvas/84 × 68
Palma il Vecchio (?)
Detroit, Institute of Arts

544 Madonna and Child, St Agnes and the Infant Baptist (W.I, 103)
Oil on canvas/111 × 149
Palma il Vecchio, with Titian's assistance (Saint Agnes)
Dijon, Musée des Beaux-Arts

545 Portrait of Gentlewoman with Vase (V. 587)
Oil on canvas/99.5 × 88
Dresden, Gemäldegalerie

546 Holy Family Adored by the Donor and Members of his Household (P. 346)
Oil on canvas/118 × 161
Girolamo Dente (?)
Dresden, Gemäldegalerie

547 Sleeping Venus (W.III, 185)
Oil on canvas/108.5 × 165
Giorgione, with Titian's assistance (Cupid and landscape)
Dresden, Gemäldegalerie

548 Supper at Emmaus (W.I, 179)
Oil on canvas/162 × 199
Dublin, National Gallery of Ireland

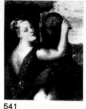

541

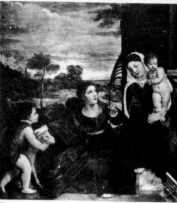
544

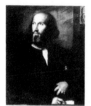
542

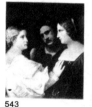

543

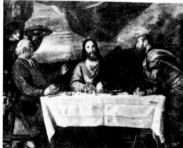
546

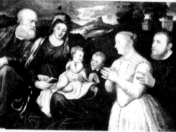
545

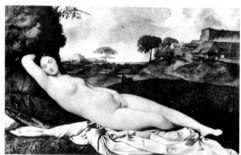
548

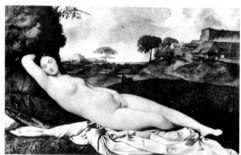
547

Self-portrait (No. 458)
Possibly Titian's last 'formal' self-portrait, sent in all probability to Philip II during the 1570s. At that time the artist was probably already eighty years old, and he has portrayed himself with merciless accuracy.

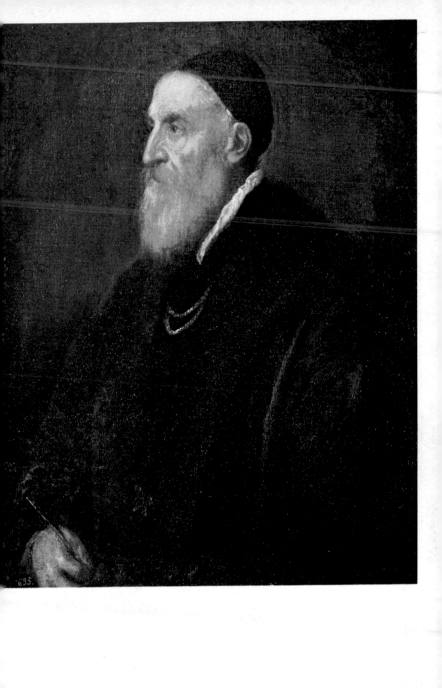

549 St Mary Magdalene with St Blaise, Tobias and the Angel, and Donor (W.I, 151)
Oil on canvas/208 × 163
Dubrovnik, Church of San Domenico

550 Mathias Hofer (W.II, 170)
Oil on canvas/121 × 88
Gian Paolo Pase (?)
Duino, Castello Nuovo, Collection of Principi della Torre e Tassi
Not illustrated

551 Venus, Mercury and Cupid (The Education of Cupid) (W.III, 223)
Oil on canvas/180 × 115
Sustris (?)
El Paso, Museum of Art

552 Rest on the Flight into Egypt (W.I, 125)
Oil on canvas/155 × 323
Sustris (?)
Escorial, Nuevos Museos

553 Madonna and Child with St Dorothy (W.I, 108)
Oil on canvas/115 × 150
Girolamo Dente (?)
Philadelphia, Museum of Art

554 Resurrection (W.I, 177)
Oil on canvas/133 × 82
Florence, Contini Bonacossi Collection

555 Bust of Christ (W.I, 78)
Oil on panel/77 × 57
Copy (?)
Florence, Pitti Palace

556 Madonna of Mercy (W.I, 114)
Oil on canvas/154 × 144
Marco Vecellio (?)
Florence, Pitti Palace

557 Andreas Vesalius (W.II, 187)
Oil on canvas/128 × 98
Florence, Pitti Palace

Tarquin and Lucretia (No. 459)
The theme of Tarquin and Lucretia occupied the ageing Titian several times (see the Cambridge and Bordeaux versions (Nos 460 and 461)). The Vienna sketch may possibly be for this latter canvas, so piercingly lifelike, with the gleams of light emphasizing the planes of colour.

549

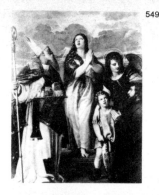
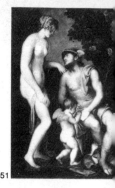

551

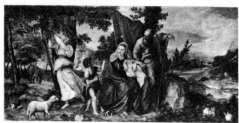

552

553

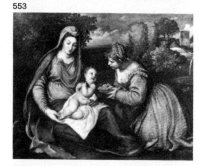

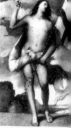

554

556

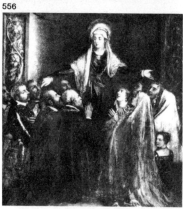

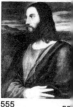

555

55

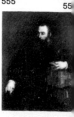

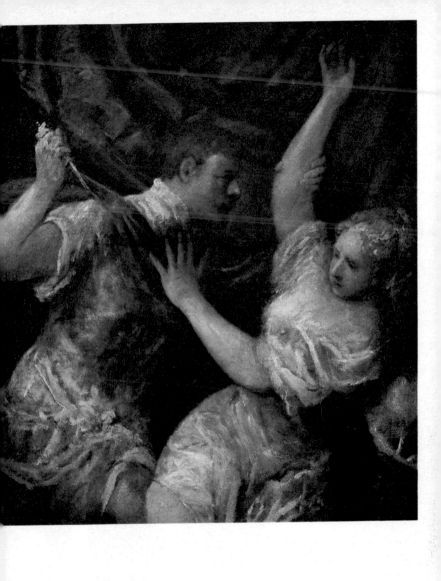

558 Diego Hurtado de Mendoza (incorrectly called) (W.II, 110)
Oil on canvas/179 × 114
Florence, Pitti Palace
559 A Gentleman Seated (W.II, 168)
Oil on canvas/129 × 98
Florence, Pitti Palace
560 Madonna and Child with Infant Baptist (W.I, 176)
Oil on canvas/100 × 83
Marco Vecellio (?)
Florence, Uffizi
Not illustrated
561 Portrait of Giovanni de'Medici (W.II, 173)
Oil on canvas/90 × 97
Gian Paolo Pase
Florence, Uffizi
Not illustrated
562 Portrait of a Senator
Oil on panel/74.5 × 59
Bonifacio Veronese (?)
Florence, Uffizi
Not illustrated
563 Sixtus IV (W.II, 140)
Oil on panel/110 × 90
Florence, Uffizi
564 Portrait of a Man (V. 56)
Oil on canvas/81 × 60
Sebastiano del Piombo (?)
Florence, Uffizi
565 St Catherine of Alexandria (W.I, 130)
Oil on panel/102.5 × 72
Marco Vecellio (?)
Florence, Uffizi
566 Young Man in a Red Cap (W.II, 150)
Oil on panel/19 × 15
Frankfurt, Städelsches Kunstinstitut
567 St Mary Magdalene in Penitence (W.I, 149)
Oil on canvas/111 × 78
Variant of No. 392
Genoa, Palazzo Durazzo-Pallavicini
Not illustrated
568 An Elderly Patrician (W.II, 160)
Oil on canvas/92 × 78
Genoa, Palazzo Rosso
569 A Gentleman (so-called Raphael) (W.II, 166)
Oil on canvas/82.5 × 64.5
Geneva, Filiginetti Collection

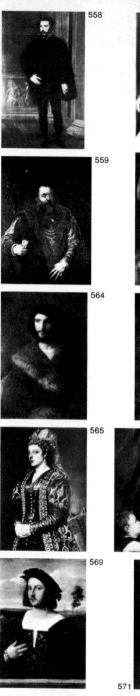
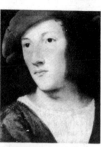
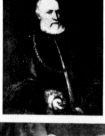
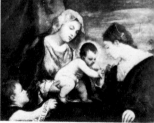
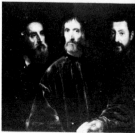

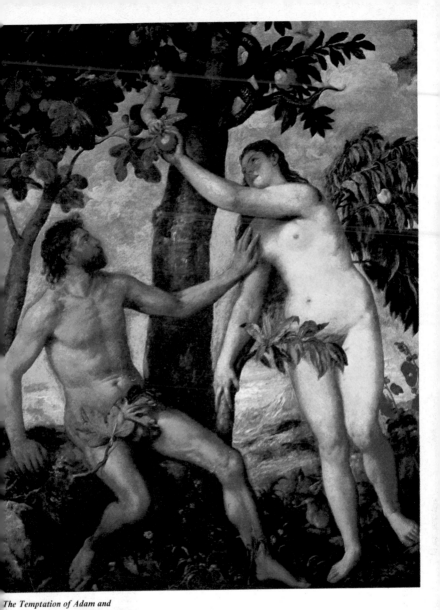

The Temptation of Adam and Eve (No. 462)
In the positioning of the figures Titian was only superficially inspired by Michelangelo. Once again he is using the coloured planes typical of his last works, with their subtle interplay of light and shadow.

570 Madonna and Child, with St Catherine and the Infant Baptist (W.I, 174)
Oil on canvas/75.6 × 97.8
Francesco Vecellio (?)
Hampton Court, Royal Collection
571 Titian, Andrea dei Franceschi and the Friend of Titian (W.II, 183)
Oil on canvas/80.5 × 93
Hampton Court, Royal Collection
572 Pomponio Vecellio (so-called) (W.II, 185)
Oil on canvas/107.3 × 86
Kreuzlingen, Kisters Collection
Not illustrated
573 A Gentleman with a Long Beard (W.II, 167)
Oil on canvas/98.3 × 74.2
Kreuzlingen, Kisters Collection
574 Andrea de' Franceschi (W.II, 164)
Oil on canvas/86.5 × 68.5
Variant of No. 137
Indianapolis, G. H. A. Clowes Collection
575 A Gentleman with Flashing Eyes (W.II, 104)
Oil on canvas/77.4 × 63.5
Cariani (?)
Ickworth, Bury St Edmunds (National Trust)
576 Christ Giving his Blessing (P. 274)
Oil on canvas/72.5 × 65
London, Viscount Darnley Collection
577 A Gentleman (V. 71)
Oil on canvas/81 × 68.5
London, Duke of Devonshire Collection
578 The Triumph of Love (W.III, 220)
Oil on canvas/diam. 85
London, McKenna Collection
579 Venus and Wounded Cupid (W.III, 224)
Oil on canvas/111 × 139
Francesco Vecellio (?)
London, Wallace Collection
580 Giovanni Francesco Acquaviva d' Aragona (W.II, 151)
Oil on canvas/140 × 102
Lucerne, Böhler Collection
581 Cardinal (W.II, 157)
Oil on canvas/111 × 91
Lucerne, private collection

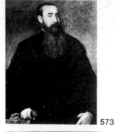

573

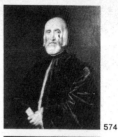

574

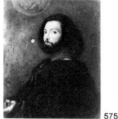

575

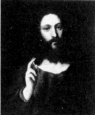

576

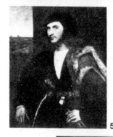

577

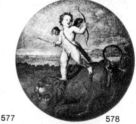

578

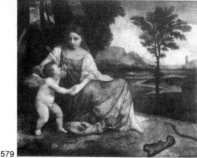

579

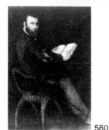

580

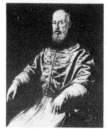

581

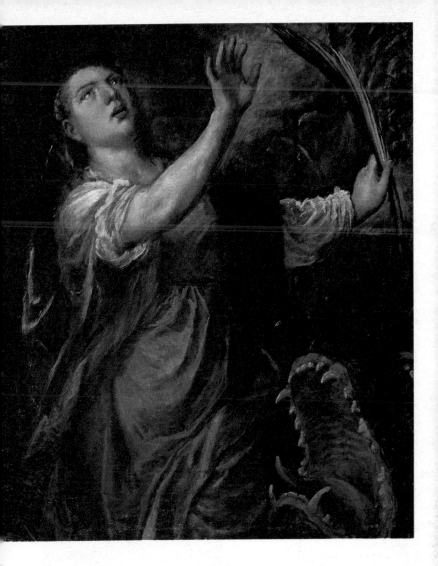

St Margaret (No. 465)
Reattributed to Titian as a
result of recent restoration, St
Margaret rises from the
greenish shadow, fleeing the
sea monster, to soar upwards
towards the light. This late
masterpiece seems to betray
some deep anxiety which has
caused the painter's brush to
tremble.

79

582 The Adoration of the Kings (W.I, 66)
Oil on canvas/141 × 219
Variant of No. 385
Madrid, Prado
Not illustrated

583 Christ carrying the Cross (W.I, 80)
Oil on canvas/98 × 116
Madrid, Prado

584 Ecce Homo (V. 499)
Oil on canvas/100 × 100
Variant of No. 476
Madrid, Prado

585 A Gentleman in a Lynx Collar (W.II, 168)
Oil on canvas/81 × 68
Madrid, Prado

586 St Margaret (W.I, 178)
Oil on canvas/116 × 91
Madrid, Prado
Not illustrated

587 The Adoration of the Kings (W.I, 64)
Oil on canvas/118 × 222
Variant of No. 385
Milan, Pinacoteca Ambrosiana

588 Landscape with two Satyrs and a Nymph (W.III, 214)
Oil on panel/30.7 × 77.5
In poor condition
Milan, private collection

589 Lady with Pearl Necklace (W.II, 172)
Oil on canvas/90 × 75
Milan, private collection

590 A Warrior (W.II, 188)
Oil on canvas/94 × 73.3
Milan, formerly in Chiesa Collection
Not illustrated

591 Madonna and Child, with SS Francis, Jerome, and Anthony Abbot (W.I, 175)
Oil on canvas/100 × 137
Francesco Vecellio (?)
Munich, Alte Pinakothek

Faith Adored by Doge Antonio Grimani (No. 466; detail)
Intended for the Sala delle Quattro Porte in the Ducal Palace, only a delay in delivery saved it from the fire of 1574. After Titian's death Marco Vecellio finished the figures on the right, but Titian's own touch has, in the recent restoration, re-emerged in the marvellous central figures.

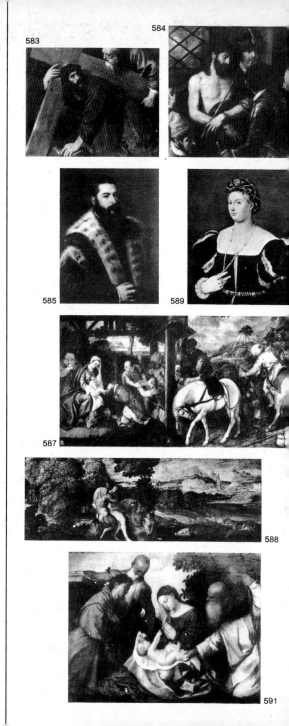

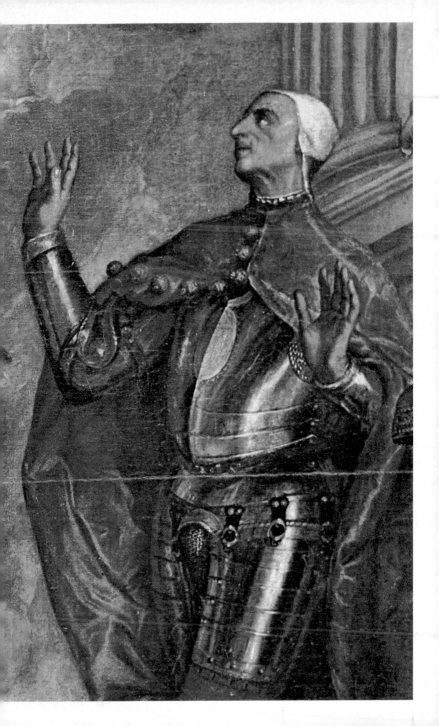

592 A Knight of Santiago
(W.II, 113)
Oil on canvas/139.5 × 117.5
Munich, Alte Pinakothek
Penitence (W.I, 145)
*593 St Mary Magdalene in
Penitence* (W.I, 145)
Oil on canvas/128 × 103
Variant of No. 392
Naples, Galleria Nazionale di
Capodimonte
594 Portrait of Ferdinand I(?)
(W.II, J57)
Oil on canvas/99 × 74
Naples, Galleria Nazionale di
Capodimonte
595 Pierluigi Farnese (W.II,
161)
Oil on panel/100 × 75
Naples, Royal Palace
*596 Guidobaldo II della
Rovere, Duke of Urbino*
(W.II, 177)
Oil on canvas/62.3 × 42.8
New Haven, Yale University
Art Gallery
Not reproduced
597 Danaë with Cupid (W.III,
132)
Oil on canvas/105.5 × 162.6
Variant of No. 255
New York, Golovin
Collection
598 Vincenzo Cappello (W.II,
83)
Oil on canvas/135 × 115
Variant of No. 193
New York, P. Chrysler Jr
Collection
Not reproduced
599 Father and Son (W.II,
163)
Oil on canvas/123 × 96
Padua, private collection
600 Adoration of the Magi
(V. 425)
Oil on canvas/217 × 149
Variant of No. 385
Faris, d'Atri Collection
Not reproduced
601 Man with a Sword (W.II,
173)
Oil on canvas/99 × 82
Tintoretto
Paris, Louvre
*602 Madonna and Child, with
SS Roch and Sebastian* (W.I,
177)
Oil on canvas/180 × 220
Francesco Vecellio (?)
Pieve di Cadore, Parish
Church

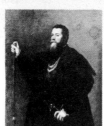

592

594

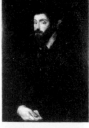

593

595

599

601

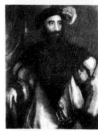

602

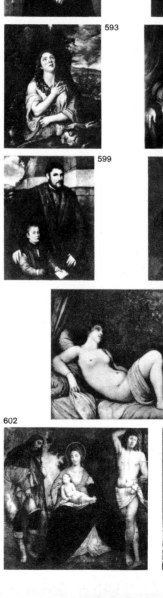

597

6

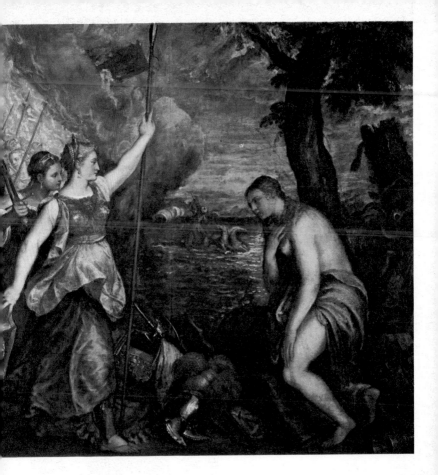

Religion Succoured by Spain
(No. 470)

Titian worked on a Triumph
of Virtue over Vice *for
Alfonso, Duke of Este, which
was still not completed in
1534, and indeed was never
delivered. He resumed work on
it for Philip II only after 1571,
transforming it into the
present canvas, which
combines a design from his
early years with the dull glow
of his late colours.*

603 Madonna and Child, with the Infant Baptist (V. 23)
Oil on canvas/75 × 62
Sante Zago (?)
Formerly Richmond, Cook Collection

ROGANZUOLO TRIPTYCH (W.I, 112)
(Nos 604A–604D)
Workshop of Titian
Roganzuolo, Parish Church
604A Madonna and Child
Oil on canvas/240 × 80
604B St Paul
Oil on canvas/190 × 57
604C St Peter
Oil on canvas/190 × 57
604D Dead Christ Supported by an Angel
Oil on canvas/80 × 80
Not reproduced

605 Ippolito Riminaldi (W.II, 177)
Oil on canvas/116 × 93
Orazio Vecellio (?)
Rome, Accademia di San Luca
Not reproduced
606 Madonna and Child (W.I, 100)
Oil on canvas/122.5 × 94
Rome, Albertini Collection
Not reproduced
607 Flagellation (W.I, 93)
Oil on canvas/86 × 58
Rome, Borghese Gallery
608 Angel with Tambourine (V. 25)
Oil on canvas/98.5 × 66.5
Sante Zago (?)
Rome, Galleria Doria
609 Sacra Conversazione (V. 24)
Oil on panel/83 × 113
Sante Zago (?)
Rome, Galleria Doria

A Boy with Dogs (No. 474; detail)
A stormy sky seems to envelop the background of this canvas, a work of Titian's last period, in the shadows of approaching night. The colour, in a range of low tones, has a shining luminescence as if damp surfaces have been washed by recent rain.

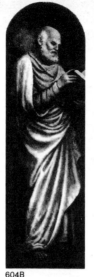

604A

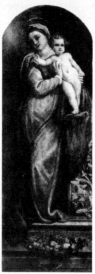

604B

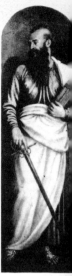

60

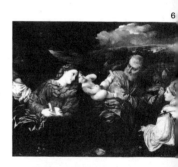

6

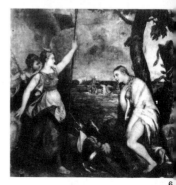

6

607

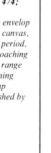

608

611

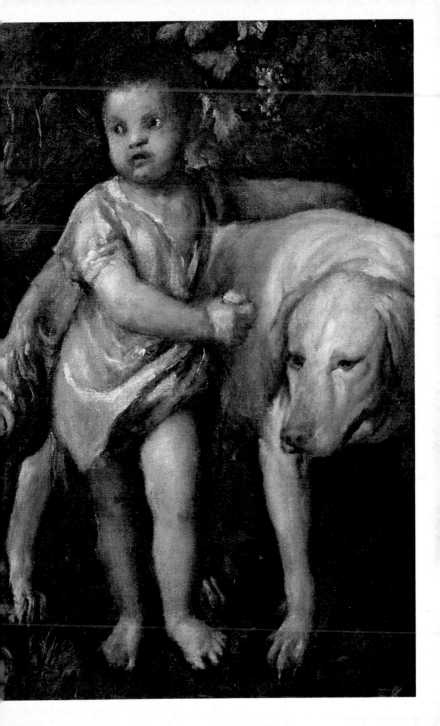

610 Religion Succoured by Spain (W.I, 124)
Oil on canvas/168 × 172
Variant of No. 470
Rome, Galleria Doria
611 Philip II (W.II, 131)
Oil on canvas/108 × 78
Rome, National Gallery.

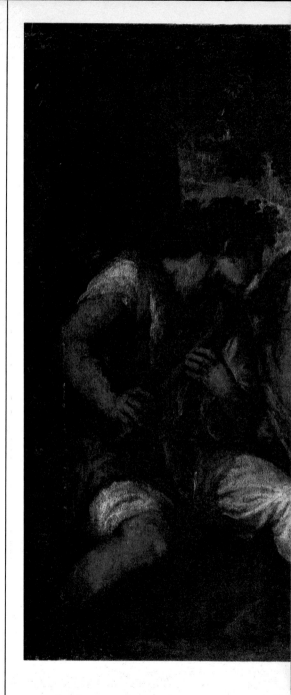

Nymph and Shepherd
(**No. 475**)
*One of the most evocative of
Titian's late works, its poetic
mood touched by chill. In his
last period – according to
Palma's evidence – he worked
impulsively, sometimes
modelling the colour with his
fingertips.*

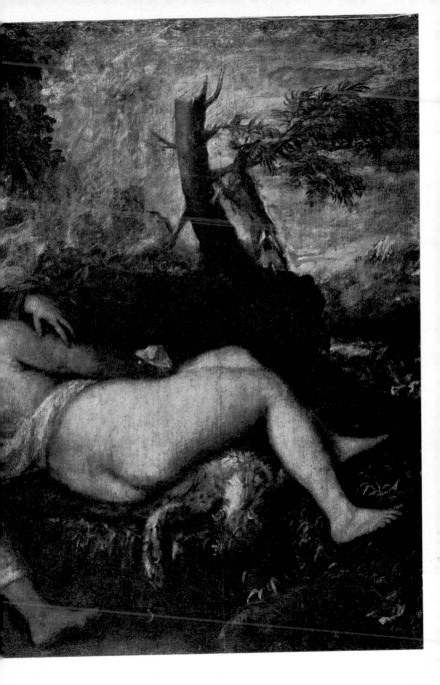

612 St Mary Magdalene in Penitence (P. 325)
Oil on panel/111 × 79
Variant of No. 135
Rome, private collection

613 Nymph and Faun (W.III, 216)
Oil on canvas/63 × 53.5
Rotterdam, Museum Boymans-van Beuningen

614 Madonna and Child, with the Infant Baptist (W.I, 176)
Oil on canvas/67 × 55
Francesco Vecellio (?)
San Diego, Fine Arts Gallery

615 Venetian Gentleman (W.II, 186)
Oil on canvas/94 × 70
San Paolo, Museu de Arte

616 Madonna and Child (P. 346)
Oil on panel/172.5 × 79.5
Francesco Vecellio (?)
Sedico, Parish Church

617 St Mary Magdalene in Penitence (W.I, 146)
Oil on canvas/144 × 99
Variant of No. 392
Stuttgart, Staatsgalerie

618 St Mark (W.I, 179)
Mosaic/320 × 180
Cartoon by Titian
Venice, St Mark's Basilica

619 St Geminianus (V. 169)
Mosaic/215 × 90
Cartoon by Titian (?)
Venice, St Mark's Basilica

620 Pope St Clement
Mosaic
Cartoon by Titian (?)
Venice, Porch of St Mark's Basilica
Not reproduced

621 Saints
Mosaic
Cartoons by Titian (?)
Venice, Sacristy of St Mark's Basilica
Not reproduced

622 Transfiguration (W.I, 163)
Oil on canvas/245 × 295
Workshop of Titian
Venice, Church of San Salvador

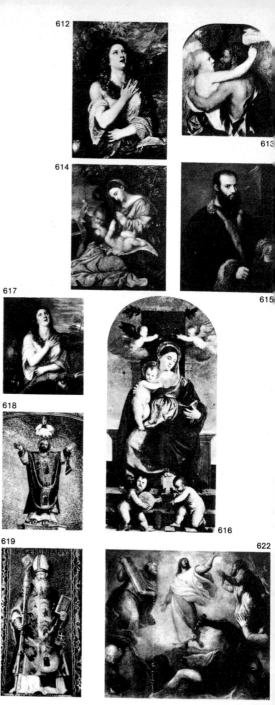

612

613

614

615

617

618

619

616

622

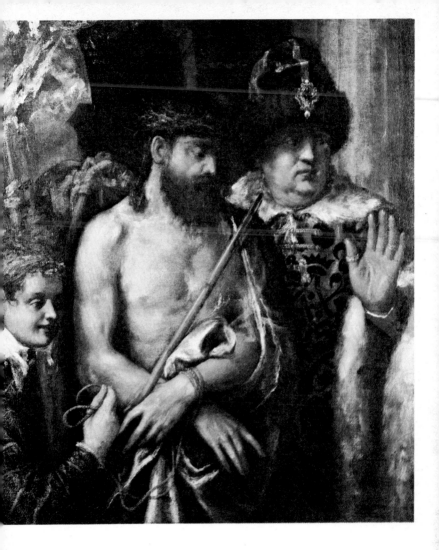

Christ Mocked (*No. 476*)
*Titian painted numerous
versions of this particularly
expressive composition, of
which this one, in Saint Louis,
is probably the finest. Its
tormented colour seems an
indication of the distress of the
old master.*

***Christ Crowned with Thorns
(No. 478)***
*With this very late
masterpiece, Titian repeated a
subject he had already
executed thirty years earlier
for Santa Maria delle Grazie
in Milan (No. 230). Here the
light comes only from the
torch, and falls like a rain of
fire on the figures glimmering
in the shadows beneath.*

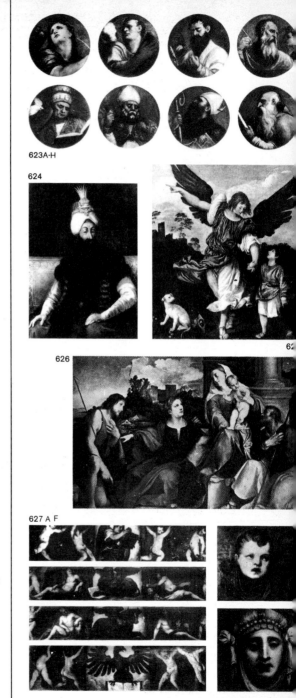

623A-H

624

62[...]

626

627 A F

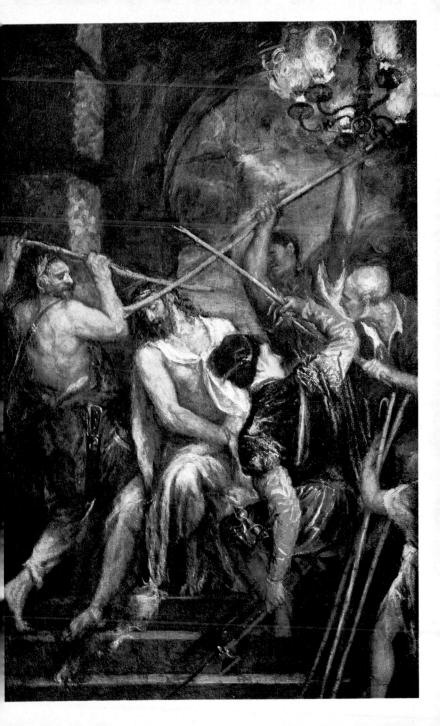

PANELS FROM THE SCUOLA DI SAN GIOVANNI EVANGELISTA (W.I, 138)
(Nos 627A–627F)
Workshop of Titian
Venice, Accademia
627A Cupid's Heads (8)
Oil on panel/39.4 × 44.5 each
627B Grotesques (8)
Oil on panel/44 × 48 each
627C Symbol of Matthew the Evangelist
Oil on panel/49.3 × 203.5
627D Symbol of Mark the Evangelist
Oil on panel/45.7 × 241
627E Symbol of Luke the Evangelist
Oil on panel/46 × 203.5
627F Symbol of John the Evangelist
Oil on panel/49.5 × 198

628 Christ Carrying the Cross (W.I, 80)
Oil on canvas/70 × 100
Giorgione
Venice, Scuola di San Rocco
629 Man of Sorrows (W.I, 115)
Oil on canvas/56 × 81
Giorgione's circle
Venice, Scuola di San Rocco
630 Adoration of the Shepherds (W.I, 168)
Oil on canvas/91 × 115
Vienna, Kunsthistorisches Museum
Not reproduced
631 Christ and the Adulteress (W.I, 77)
Oil on canvas/106 × 137
Workshop of Titian
Vienna, Kunsthistorisches Museum
632 Diana and Callisto (W.III, 142)
Oil on canvas/183 × 200
Girolamo Dente (?)
Variant of No. 387
Vienna, Kunsthistorisches Museum

633 Cupid with Tambourine (W.III, 208)
Oil on canvas/51.7 × 51
Francesco Vecellio (?)
Vienna, Kunsthistorisches Museum

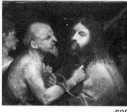
628

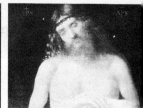
62

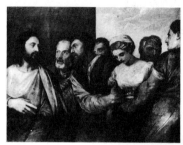
631

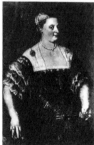
634

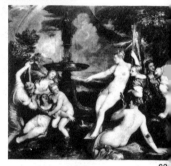
63

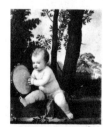
633

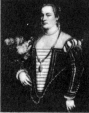
635

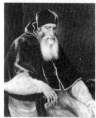
636

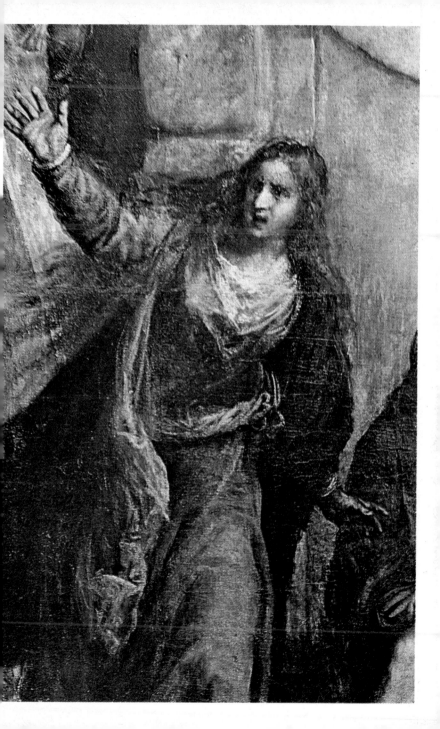

634 Caterina Cornaro (?)
(W.II, 159)
Oil on canvas/124 × 82
Antonio Badile (?)
Vienna, Kunsthistorisches
Museum
635 Lavinia as Matron (so-
called) (?) (W.II, 172)
Oil on canvas/111.5 × 90
Vienna, Kunsthistorisches
Museum
636 Paul III with Cap (W.II,
124)
Oil on canvas/89 × 78
Copy of No. 249
Vienna, Kunsthistorisches
Museum
637 Bust of Christ (W.I, 79)
Oil on canvas/82.5 × 60.5
Vienna, Kunsthistorisches
Museum
Not reproduced
*638 Madonna and Child
appearing to SS Peter and
Andrew* (W.I, 112)
Oil on canvas/456 × 270
Workshop of Titian
Vittorio Veneto, Duomo
*639 Cupid with Wheel of
Fortune* (W.III, 209)
Oil on canvas/66 × 55
Washington, National
Gallery of Art
640 Feast of the Gods (W.III,
143)
Oil on canvas/167.5 × 185
Giovanni Bellini, with
Titian's assistance for the
landscape
Washington, National
Gallery of Art
*641 Madonna and Child, with
the Infant Baptist* (W.I, 176)
Oil on canvas/28 × 58
Washington, National
Gallery of Art
642 Andrea de'Franceschi
(W.II, 101)
Oil on canvas/65 × 51
Variant of No. 137
Washington, National
Gallery of Art
643 Emilia di Spilimbergo
(W.II, 178)
Oil on canvas/122 × 106
Gian Paolo Pase
Washington, National
Gallery of Art
644 Irene da Spilimbergo
(W.II, 178)
Oil on canvas/122 × 106.5
Gian Paolo Pase (?)
Washington, National
Gallery of Art

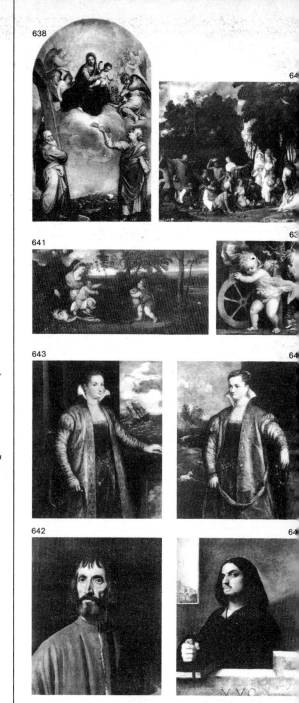

638

640

639

641

643

644

642

645

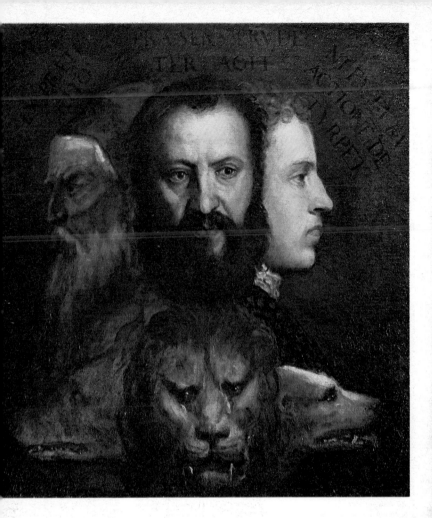

Pietà (No. 479; detail)
(p. 93)
*Intended by Titian to decorate
his tomb in the Cappella del
Crocefisso in the Frari, it
could not actually be placed
there on the death of Titian in
1576. The Magdalene's
desperate cry has a sinister
ring in the light that bathes the
architectural background and
the ghostly statues.*

Allegory of Prudence
(No. 480)
*According to Panofsky's
interesting hypothesis, this
may have been the lid of a
casket belonging to Titian's
household. The old artist
portrayed himself on it,
together with his son Orazio
and his grandson Marco, as
symbols of the three ages of
man.*

Select Bibliography

Sources

ARETINO P: *Lettere sull' arte di Pietro Aretino*, commentary by Pertile E. and edited by Camesasca (Milan, 1960).

CICOGNA E. A.: *Della iscrizioni veneziane* (Venice, 1824–53).

CLOULAS A: 'Documents concernant Titien conservés aux Archives de Simancas' in *Melanges de la Casa de Velázquez* (Madrid, 1967, pp. 197–286).

FABBRO C: *Tiziano* (Belluno, 1968).

FERRARINO L: *Tiziano e la corte di Spagna* (Madrid, 1975).

GANDINI C: *Tiziano. Le lettere* (Belluno, 1977).

LORENZI G. B: *Monumentii per servire alla storia del Palazzo Ducale di Venezia* (Venice, 1868).

MICHIEL M. A: *Notizia d'opera e di disegno*, 1521–43 (edition Frizzoni, Bologna, 1884)

POZZA N: *Tiziano* (Milan, 1976).

RIDOLFI C: *Le Maraviglie dell' Arte* (Venice, 1648, edited by Von Hadeen H., Berlin, 1914–24).

SANSOVINO F: *Venezia città nobilissima . . .* (Venice, 1581).

SANUTO M: *Diarii 1496–1533* (Venice, 1879–1902).

VASARI G: *Le vite dei più eccelenti Pittori . . .* (Florence, 1568, edited by Ragghianti C. L., Milan, 1942–9).

VASARI G: The Lives of the painters, sculptors and architects . . . (English edition edited with an introduction by Gaunt W., London, 1963).

Critical Studies

BERENSON B: *Italian Pictures of the Renaissance, Venetian School* (London, 1957).

CAGLI C., with the catalogue of Valcanover F: *Tiziano* (Milan, 1969).

CAVALCASELLE G. B., CROWE J. A: *Tiziano, la sua vita e i suoi tempi* (Florence, 1877–8) translated as *Life and Times of Titian* (London, 1877, 1881).

GRONAU G: Titian (English translation, London, 1904).

HOURTICQ L: *La jeunesse de Titien* (Paris, 1919).

LONGHI R: 'Cartella Tizianesca', in *Vita Artistica* (1927, pp. 216–26).

LONGHI R: 'Giunte a Tiziano' in *L'Arte* (1925, pp. 40–5).

MORASSI A: *Tiziano* (Milan, 1964).

MURARO M., ROSAND D: *Tiziano e la silografia veneziana del '500* (Venice, 1976).

OBERHUBER K: *Disegni di Tiziano* (Venice, 1976).

PALLUCCHINI R: *Tiziano* (Florence, 1969).

PANOFSKY E: *Problems in Titian, mostly Iconographic* (London, 1969).

PIGNATTI T: *I disegni di Tiziano* (Florence, 1979).

REARICK W. R.: *Tiziano e il disegno venezian* (Florence, 1976).

SUIDA W: *Tiziano* (Rome, 1933).

TIETZE H: *Titian* (London, 1950).

Tiziano e il Manierismo Europeo, Atti de Convegno (Venice, 1978).

Tiziano e Venezia, Atti del Convegno (Venice 1979).

VALCANOVER F: *Titian* (London, 1965).

VALCANOVER F: *L'opera completa di Tiziano* (Milan 1969).

WETHEY H. E: *Titian* (London, 1969–75).

First published in Great Britain by Granada Publishing 1981
Frogmore, St Albans, Herts AL2 2NF

Copyright © Rizzoli Editore 1979
This translation copyright
© Granada Publishing 1981

ISBN (hardback) 0 246 11298 0
ISBN (paperback) 0 586 05148 1

Printed in Italy

Granada ®
Granada Publishing ®